STORIES
from THE
HEART
Vol.1

STORIES *from* THE HEART

Vol.1

J. D. Dennis

XULON ELITE

Xulon Press
555 Winderley Pl, Suite 225
Maitland, FL 32751
407.339.4217
www.xulonpress.com

Xulon Elite

© 2025 by J. D. Dennis

All rights reserved solely by the author. The author guarantees all contents are original and do not infringe upon the legal rights of any other person or work. No part of this book may be reproduced in any form without the permission of the author.

Due to the changing nature of the Internet, if there are any web addresses, links, or URLs included in this manuscript, these may have been altered and may no longer be accessible. The views and opinions shared in this book belong solely to the author and do not necessarily reflect those of the publisher. The publisher therefore disclaims responsibility for the views or opinions expressed within the work.

Unless otherwise indicated, Scripture quotations taken from the Holy Bible, New International Version (NIV). Copyright © 1973, 1978, 1984, 2011 by Biblica, Inc.™. Used by permission. All rights reserved.

Unless otherwise indicated, Scripture quotations taken from the English Standard Version® (ESV). (The Holy Bible, English Standard Version®), © 2001 by Crossway, a publishing ministry of Good News Publishers. Used by permission. All rights reserved..

Paperback ISBN-13: 979-8-86850-953-7
Hard Cover ISBN-13: 979-8-86850-954-4
Ebook ISBN-13: 979-8-86850-955-1

STORIES
from THE
HEART

Vol.1

J. D. Dennis

XULON ELITE

Xulon Press
555 Winderley Pl, Suite 225
Maitland, FL 32751
407.339.4217
www.xulonpress.com

Exulon
  LITE

© 2025 by J. D. Dennis

All rights reserved solely by the author. The author guarantees all contents are original and do not infringe upon the legal rights of any other person or work. No part of this book may be reproduced in any form without the permission of the author.

Due to the changing nature of the Internet, if there are any web addresses, links, or URLs included in this manuscript, these may have been altered and may no longer be accessible. The views and opinions shared in this book belong solely to the author and do not necessarily reflect those of the publisher. The publisher therefore disclaims responsibility for the views or opinions expressed within the work.

Unless otherwise indicated, Scripture quotations taken from the Holy Bible, New International Version (NIV). Copyright © 1973, 1978, 1984, 2011 by Biblica, Inc.™. Used by permission. All rights reserved.

Unless otherwise indicated, Scripture quotations taken from the English Standard Version® (ESV). (The Holy Bible, English Standard Version®), © 2001 by Crossway, a publishing ministry of Good News Publishers. Used by permission. All rights reserved..

Paperback ISBN-13: 979-8-86850-953-7
Hard Cover ISBN-13: 979-8-86850-954-4
Ebook ISBN-13: 979-8-86850-955-1

Dedication:

This book is dedicated to my family and friends, without whom this would not have been possible. This has been a long time in the making, and each one of you has walked with me through this period in one spot or another. To my husband, thank you for being the amazing man of God that you are to me, our children, and our grandchildren. You are truly a gift straight from the Father's heart. To our beautiful babies, first I thank God for my "rainbow" children J and C; without you my life would have been hollow and empty, and yes, very quiet! Love y'all. To the spiritual children, you are a constant reminder of the goodness of God in my life. To the friends who were and those who are now, God bless you.

To Mary Catherine, thank you for being my ride or die, my BFF and for laughing with me, crying with me, and being an incredible friend. I cannot imagine my life without you in it. Thank you for then, and for the days to come. Some friends have moved on in life, but what you gave, I will cherish and honor always. To my siblings and my mom and dad, what a ride, huh? I love you and dedicate a portion of this to you! To all you have poured into my walk and life, I dedicate this first book to you. I pray and believe there is much more to come and to share! To my Gina, you have no idea how much your patience and comforting talks have meant to me. I couldn't not put you in my dedication; I appreciate you so much! Love and blessings to you all! Blessed to be a blessing, and a blessing wherever I go!

Contents

Preface xi
Map of Words xv

MINI READ 1. 1
Scream Savers and Bumper Stickers!

MINI READ 2. 7
A Mess in Progress

MINI READ 3. 13
Sometimes I Get Mad at God

MINI READ 4. 19
God Is Watching

MINI READ 5. 25
What Would You Have Me Say, Father?

MINI READ 6. 31
The "Ish" of Life

MINI READ 7. 37
When It Hurts, Cry

MINI READ 8. 43
Sticks and Stones

MINI READ 9. 57
Supernatural Expectations

MINI READ 10. 67
The God We Created

MINI READ 11. 73
  If I Lived in This World

MINI READ 12. 79
  The Freedom of Forgiveness

Mini Read 13 85
  The Weirdest Lonely I Have Ever Known

Mini Read 14 Includes "Super-Mini's" 93
  I Almost didn't finish! Feeling All The feels, Why not just Quit?

Preface

As you read, you may notice the ellipses (. . .), and I want to share with you what those mean to me. Well, in my head I have already been having a conversation with God or myself, and now I am just starting in the middle of a conversation that now includes you. You know those folks who just start talking to you about anything, and you're like, "What are we talking about?" It's also like a pause you might say. Well, that happens to me a lot, and I wanted you to know why you might see the ellipses and be privy to why they're there. You know, as I get my downloads from heaven, or my assignments. I like to say from the Father in heaven to write, I am not really writing to or for any one person as much and even more so than I am writing for myself, to remember God's goodness. It has occurred to me as I live and breathe, as I move about in life, I just don't have all the answers. I can't seem to grasp what some folks seem to easily do; I feel simple in my understanding of God and His glorious word sometimes! Heck, I feel that way about life! I sometimes feel small, or way out in left field, so to speak, in how I see and experience God at times. And do you know what I found out? That it's okay!

I believe that's just how God the Heavenly Father of all that is good communicates with me. He does so on a very basic level—real, honest, and raw in verbiage and expression to and with me! I know that my terms and terminology may offend some; for that, my apologies up front. Others may applaud. Honestly, I am not really looking for either; I only want to share what is in my heart and my perspective. Although some of these stories—or MINIs, as I call them—may come from people past and present and experiences in my life. I post no names of these beautiful people, though. At least not without permission. I do know and understand that my ability to write and share them comes straight from God. I am just not that talented on my own. The desire to write comes straight from the Heart of God, for which I am honored and grateful.

It is okay if you choose to disagree with the book, get angry at it, throw it down, cry, and/or even stop reading it for a while; all these responses will be appropriate depending on your day and what is happening in "your" life while you are reading. I do hope, though, that you will search some of these things out for yourself as they pertain to you and your life, your world, and maybe some of your struggles and your victories. Don't just read it as *Stories from the Heart* but as stories that impact your heart. Remember these are testimonies of things that have happened in my life and world. So I am being real and vulnerable in sharing.

You see, in writing these MINIs about who God is to me, I believe that they shouldn't just be for those of us who know Him! Yes, I mean God! They aren't only for those who already have a personal and intimate relationship with Him, or even those who say they know Him! Or those who think they do. I pray that these MINIs are to be shared with all. The Pre-Cs (new Christians) might think that just 'cause we "USNs" or Christians or Christ Followers have a relationship with Him, we don't face hard times and real-life challenges. Many of our struggles are no different from those had by people who have not yet received "the free gift." Well, it rains on everyone when it's raining! The advantage we have is we have received and accepted Jesus! No matter what, we should always remember that Jesus is our ultimate destination.

I hope that the Pre-Cs who read these MINIs will be intrigued by a loving, caring, "Awesome" Creator—enough to investigate who He is for themselves, meaning read the "word" of the Bible for themselves, not just taking my word or anyone else's, for that matter. That they find out He isn't out to "smash and crash" them because of their imperfections but to love them so much He causes them to fall in love with themselves and Him and Him being God for the first time, and in a way they have yet to experience. It's exhilarating and freeing!

Love them back to their "Original Intent" in Him! To go out and live an extraordinary life daily! Hey, and even if you are living a good life, wouldn't it be awesome to live a Godly one? It sincerely could be, you know! One without anxiety, shame, or dishonor but won over by, with, and for love, living in full acceptance, forgiveness, and total freedom and liberty! And no, it doesn't mean no bad days. But it still means living prosperously—mind, spirit, and body—and full of every good thing you need!

Here is something I have come across is many Pre-C's; they believe that to give themselves over to Papa God means to give up their fun days, that we "true believers" (because everyone eventually believes in something) don't party hard. Well, that just ain't true—the best days with Papa God are yet to come. By the way, in case you didn't know, here are some facts for all y'all: There isn't any partying in hell—only pain, torment, and eternal suffering. I'm not trying to scare anyone; just stating the facts as they are written in the Bible . . . the choice is always yours. Please, please keep reading on!

My MINIs are not by any means meant to condemn anyone for any reason or for anything. That would be considered judging you, and I do not have the right to do that, nor do I ever want to! I write to offer a different perspective offered of a loving and caring Creator that I have personally experienced. Because I believe if we go around condemning one another, where's the love in that? True love covers all kinds of mistakes and boo-boos and leads to actual life change. Besides, we may have to come to an agreement to agree or disagree, but that doesn't mean I don't agape you. Believe me, I do! I do agape you!

Oh, yes, let me briefly explain a few words I use constantly; it will help you get where I am coming from in my perspective:

Map of Words (Glossary)

Pre-Cs = Those who have not yet confessed to Jesus their love and acceptance of who He is and what He has done for them! In other words, they're not Christians yet. Remember, resistance is futile because *love* is gonna getcha! :).

God = God, Papa God, Papa, Father, Daddy God, Heavenly Father, the Creator Loving Lord, the Triune God, the One, Holy One, Him.

Jesus = Jesus, Best BFF, Savior, Big Brother, Lord, the Way.

Holy Spirit = Holy Spirit, Comforter, Conscience.

MINI Reads, MINIs, or Reads = Another term or phrase for "short stories" is all.

Super MINIs = Super stories written within a MINI with a heading. Some Super MINIs can be read as stand-alone pieces that can be read out of context of the main story and still be understood.

Overcoming, Overcoming Challenge(s) = Your right to choice.

So Cal = Southern California or Nor Cal =Northern California

The Enemy = Most times, this term is not capitalized, and yet there are times it will need to be to project to you, the reader, the severity of this poo-head. He is the enemy of all mankind and all of heaven.

True Believers = Those who sincerely believe Jesus is Lord and that He died for our sins, and our healing! Those who believe and accept Jesus. We believe He gave His all so that we would live! Same as Usns.

Heaven = Streets paved with gold, a holy community for believers, the Usns' eternal home. From where our ambassadorship comes.

Hell = Hell. There is no party in hell. Sometimes it is necessary for me to capitalize this word to ensure you, the reader, understand this is the place that God originally created for the enemy of all mankind, and now for those who do not choose God.

Satan = The devourer, the bad one, the loser, the accuser, the thief, poo-head; also called the enemy or the Enemy.

World = Those outside of God's loving covenant; the lost; those with no hope. Those who do not choose, or have not yet chosen, Jesus as their Lord and Savior.

Usns = Those who are true believers, who have learned to love but not condemn; we leave it up to the Holy Spirit to convict you of truth, right, and wrong.

Map of Words (Glossary)

Pre-Cs = Those who have not yet confessed to Jesus their love and acceptance of who He is and what He has done for them! In other words, they're not Christians yet. Remember, resistance is futile because *love* is gonna getcha! :).

God = God, Papa God, Papa, Father, Daddy God, Heavenly Father, the Creator Loving Lord, the Triune God, the One, Holy One, Him.

Jesus = Jesus, Best BFF, Savior, Big Brother, Lord, the Way.

Holy Spirit = Holy Spirit, Comforter, Conscience.

MINI Reads, MINIs, or Reads = Another term or phrase for "short stories" is all.

Super MINIs = Super stories written within a MINI with a heading. Some Super MINIs can be read as stand-alone pieces that can be read out of context of the main story and still be understood.

Overcoming, Overcoming Challenge(s) = Your right to choice.

So Cal = Southern California or Nor Cal =Northern California

The Enemy = Most times, this term is not capitalized, and yet there are times it will need to be to project to you, the reader, the severity of this poo-head. He is the enemy of all mankind and all of heaven.

True Believers = Those who sincerely believe Jesus is Lord and that He died for our sins, and our healing! Those who believe and accept Jesus. We believe He gave His all so that we would live! Same as Usns.

Heaven = Streets paved with gold, a holy community for believers, the Usns' eternal home. From where our ambassadorship comes.

Hell = Hell. There is no party in hell. Sometimes it is necessary for me to capitalize this word to ensure you, the reader, understand this is the place that God originally created for the enemy of all mankind, and now for those who do not choose God.

Satan = The devourer, the bad one, the loser, the accuser, the thief, poo-head; also called the enemy or the Enemy.

World = Those outside of God's loving covenant; the lost; those with no hope. Those who do not choose, or have not yet chosen, Jesus as their Lord and Savior.

Usns = Those who are true believers, who have learned to love but not condemn; we leave it up to the Holy Spirit to convict you of truth, right, and wrong.

Map of Words (Glossary)

Christian = Means "Little Christ"; those who are desperately trying to sincerely walk the walk and talk the talk but realize they need Him every second of every day to survive.

The Free Gift = Salvation; why Jesus died.

I will unapologetically capitalize any word I use to describe God; in my honoring of who He is to me, I am constantly in awe of Him and His goodness, His Love, and as of yet, I cannot figure out why He would save the likes of me! I have found honestly, without Him, I might not amount to much, but in Him, with Him, and through Him, I am all I need to be and could ever be and growing. I will always capitalize Him in my life! He is the One who loves me! But then that's just me!

I hope that as you read on, you will enjoy, laugh, cry, contemplate, and meditate on these stories and that these reads will inspire you to find out more about our Heavenly Father! How about you read His book, the most important book ever written? Yes, I'm going to say it is the Bible!

Be blessed, read, and get going in this life, because *you* rock socks!

J. D. Dennis <3
. . . blessed to be a blessing, and a blessing wherever I go . . .

Mini Read 1

Scream Savers and Bumper Stickers!
(Inspired by a bumper sticker & computer screen)

I am sure when many of you Pre-Cs are reading this posted somewhere on our car bumper stickers, our shirts, our buttons, on our "scream savers"—and yes, I meant scream savers and not screen savers because I have used my own like that from time to time . . . haven't one or two of you established seasoned believers done so as well? Well, I am sure they want to *scream* themselves! Not trying to be tough on us longtime believers, the since-I-was-born-been-in-the-faith folks, but where is the *love* in our lives? Where is the compassion? Where is the patience that is desperately needed for a lost and dying world that needs it so much? You will find that love seems to be a common theme with me. Well, that's because once we get that unconditional kind of love for ourselves and for one another, I think we will seriously be on to something big! I mean love to and for everyone! God is Love!

. . . anyway, back to my little story here . . . could this be why the world would turn to mediums or psychics or to drugs, sex, violence, or other means to explain their lives, to find meaning, *to find their destinies rather to a people sent here with ambassadorship from heaven on assignment?* Doesn't that bother you? It bugs the hell out of me . . . yeah, right on out of me. Okay here comes a serious question: How is it that the world can discuss the supernatural but not the church? We should know better than any other group out there all about it! Why? Because our God is the most amazing "Super"natural being that ever was, is, and will ever be! Our God is the Ultimate Superhero, the Ultimate Fighter, the Ultimate Lover, the Ultimate All in All.

How else could we explain someone—or, for those still searching, something—that always was, always is, and always will be? He was there then, He is here now, and before you walked into the room He was there! How can you explain someone who was with you yesterday, here with you now, and already in your future? How else can you explain someone who loves you in spite of every disgusting thing you may have ever done, said, or thought, or are going to, but loves you and wants you to get every beautiful thing He has created for you? Doesn't make sense, but this is truth! How is it that a Creator so wonderful has been excited at the thought of *you* since before time and is even more wild and crazy, mad, wonderfully in love with you now? I know some of us can't even love ourselves, so how is this possible? Regardless it is truth!

Although we are "Not of this World," we are all in it, and I believe that we are *all* in it to win it! You wanna know why? Even if you don't, I'm going to share this with you . . . because we already have everything we need to do so! Because we as a loving, kind, thoughtful, giving, caring, patient, generous people got this! I read the back of the precious book; some of you might want to cheat and read it for yourselves. It is awesome, although some of you may need an updated version, because all those *thees* and *thous* used to really throw me . . . anyway, another side rant of mine.

Wouldn't it be wonderful for us to act like the One who saved us and love everyone sincerely, especially in today's emotional climate, instead of becoming an "unintentional judge" to the world? How about we become "intentional in loving all" to the world instead. How about instead of berating folks for the ignorance of what we know is truth, we share and show love, mercy, and compassion; then maybe they will want to hear and know what we get to share. Now I know and understand that many of us are doing this already, but what about the other one or two who could use a gentle nudge? What if we accepted people for who they are, allowed everyone who wanted an opportunity to come to our meeting places—meaning churches—as they are to do just that?

Our jobs are to be a people so full of love that they can't help but want to know the reason why we are the way we are.

. . . basically, I would like for all of us followers of Christ to be known as those people who love, to be those cheesy uh oh, here comes the word "Christians" we so proudly call ourselves and as we should. The ones who really do have a relationship, not just a religious view of our God! Where we share with the world that honestly we make mistakes too; we say stupid, bad, mean things sometimes. Where we honestly show the world like a good parent might teach their children that when you make a mistake, you apologize and make amends. Where we don't act like we have never done anything wrong. I don't know about some of you, but my life personally hasn't always been what it is today, and even knowing all that I know, I still flub it sometimes. How about as a people of ambassadorship

of heaven, we get real with this world so they can see we are here, we are here, we are here! . . . and that we love you! We love you because we were first loved, and so were and so are we all!

Because I am kinda scared to share this with you but am going to be transparent here . . . I tell you there have been times recently when I honestly didn't want anyone to know I was a Christian because of how mean, harsh, and judgmental some of us have come across! Some of the things I have heard some USNs say or seen them do make my heart sad.

I have come to this conclusion for myself, though, that I don't have to compromise my faith, my standing, my beliefs, and "the truth" to be loving and/or accepting of other folks who may think differently than I do. . . . *My job is to love them straight to our Heavenly Papa; I have found He can do the rest!* As one of my dearest friends once told me, "Hey, sweetheart, you are not their savior, but you can love them to the one who is." I love this approach; it frees me from trying to be someone I am not, and just love the incredible people Papa God has seen fit to put in my path . . . *and as weird and crazy strange as I am, there are those who can get my train of thought, and those folks I can reach!* Maybe I'll never have a public pulpit like a pastor or bishop does, but I have my immediate sphere of influence . . . so although I am "not of this world," I can prove I am in it, and I am in it to win it, to make His name glorious, to make His name famous, to show and share His Love, well, because He did it—not just for me but for us all! So I say wear your T-shirt, and wear it proud, and loud; make sure the world sees your bumper stickers and "scream savers," and then show the world how awesome our loving heavenly Papa is by being the best example of ambassadorship ever, every day you can!

. . . become known as one of those Christians who love everywhere you go! Because that's what the world needs: Christians who love, and who love unconditionally! Let it be so!

~Meditation Moment~

A new commandment I give to you, that you love one another: just as I have loved you, you also are to love each other (John 13:34, ESV).

"One word frees us of all the weight and pain in life. That word is love." Sophocles

Prayer for Today: Heavenly Father, bless me to be a blessing everywhere I go today. Bless even my mistakes to become a teachable moment not only to me but to those around me, to those watching me. Bless me to be one of the beautiful expressions of love and kindness You have shown to me. Bless me to be known as a peacemaker; bless me to be the hug and not the hurt in somebody's life today. Bless me to be the word of encouragement, of affirmation, today. Bless me to be a precious example of Your goodness and Your love and who You are every day! In Jesus's name I pray.

Amen!

~YOUR PRAYER OR THOUGHTS FOR TODAY~

A Mess in Progress
(Inspired by God's word)

"Out of what seemed like a big ol' mess, God created . . . and whatever God creates is good." J. D. Dennis

Hey! You know when you wake up some days and feel like everything is just off and out of sorts, so to speak. You feel like you got up on the wrong side of the bed, but your feet haven't even hit the floor yet. It's probably because yesterday was just a complete bust, and the day before that as well. Hell, actually the whole week was a mess. The days ahead aren't looking too good either. It feels like everything is a mess, and in some respects, they probably are "a mess in progress."

You go ahead and get up and go through your routine of prepping for the day or night, and then something changes in you. You say to yourself (you know that little voice in your head that feels like it is coming from your heart), "Oh, no, not today, not any day, Satan!" You hear yourself say, "I have had enough, God; please help me!" Then you know in your heart, He does just that: helps you.

Then a wonderful thing happens: You make the best cup of coffee or tea you've made in about a year. Your clothes are still warm from the dryer and wrinkle-free from the night before. Dude, your day just keeps getting better. You make every green light going and coming that day. Your boss calls you into the office to thank you for a job well-done and tells you of the promotion and pay raise that are coming your way.

It gets better. Your long-lost angry, self-centered friend calls and apologizes and asks if you two can make up. Wow! What the heck just happened? You probably desired all of this to happen anyway but didn't feel you deserved it because you knew what a mess you'd made of things.

Now let me get really real and raw with you. Let me tell you about my mess. For me personally, there have been parts of my life that should have blown up already, or I should have exploded on impact. I should never have been as blessed as I am; at least that is what some people have been all too happy to remind me of from time to time. I have screwed up so badly I am still wondering myself how I made it this far. That's when you know Papa God loves you unconditionally. I have made some grave errors, some huge mistakes, and a total mess of my life. Even as I write this, I am crying because I really have been a "not-so-good" person at times. If it were not for the love, mercy, grace, and forgiveness God has shown me and given me, and that I chose to receive, I should (and yes, I mean it) have been dead a long time ago. But thank God for being a loving and merciful God.

If the world had its way, I would be dead. Not just "the world" but the vast majority of the beloved church. Ouch— sad but true. I've had the "Scarlet Letter" placed upon my forehead by the judgments of others, and I've placed ones on others' foreheads because of my judgments of them as well. I have been shunned by people who should have stood by me, and because they wanted to stay accepted in this world, they betrayed me and left me to die instead.

I even had one who promised to protect me when we spoke our vows before God and man, then left me to be molested, harassed, and tormented by this world. I've had to struggle to get back what should never have been taken away. I've been a mess in progress and I've started a mess and not known how to fix or make it right. I have watched a mess or two happening in someone else's life and did nothing to step in and make it right on behalf of the injured party when I could have.

I tell you this much: If our Heavenly Papa, our Daddy God, can use the likes of me after all of the terrible things I have done, then He can use anyone. If He can clean me up and make me shine like Mr. Clean, if he makes me His own, takes my life, and make it so beautiful that I feel like I am in one of those fairy tale movies they used to make, then He can take your mess and bless it too. We are all His favorites, just in case you didn't know it.

You don't know where I've been. I've not been to London to look at the queen. I've been to the dark side of things—a place not seen or known to those around me. I have paid a price for some of the things I've done, yet Papa God has spared my very life in thousands of ways and too many times to number even though I was not worthy of being liked, let alone loved, according to the world's standards and my own. But then God's love got through to my heart, and this is what He said to me, and I believe if you are reading this, He is saying the same to you:

"Yes, little one, I can still use you. No, I won't abuse you, your trust, or your talents; I gave them to you. You're not disposable, you're not trash, and you're not junk. You're one of my greatest creations; you're one of my masterpieces. Your laughter brings me joy, and I treasure your smile. Though *you* and the world allowed or have caused some tragedies to come in your life, I can still use you. Although you believe you have become a mess, know this: it's not too late; it is never too late; you didn't miss it or miss out. Don't give up, don't quit, and don't throw in the towel. Don't quit; don't stop believing in yourself or in me, your heavenly Papa God.

"You, yes you, can still make a difference even if it is just with one person at a time. You can share the love I have given you with the lost and the spiritually and physically blind. You can make a difference in a world that seems to have gone mad. You can tell them, those lost ones, mean ones, hateful ones, to be quiet. You can tell them to be still and know the peace that I give."

Now you and I can say our births were not an accident. God planned "me" and "you" all along. Our lives are not a crime or a shame or a natural disaster. He called you and me and birthed us for this season, this day, and this time. If no one else ever wanted us or if no one else ever cared, even before the beginning of time as we know it, Papa God was excited about our arrival.

God declared: "They're here, they're here, they finally made it. Now they've come to Me, and they can surely make it. Please know, little ones, that now that you are in God's hands, you'll be just fine. When the obstacles come, you will beat them for sure, and it shall become an opportunity for you to glorify God.

"Your mess now blessed has become what made you powerful; it has become what grew you, and your mess still in progress now shall forever be a blessed event. It will become a recorded victory." You are blessed to a blessing, and you are a blessing wherever we go!

~MEDITATION MOMENTS ~

For this is what the Lord says—he who created the heavens, he is God; he who fashioned and made the earth, he founded it; he did not create it to be empty, but formed it to be inhabited—he says: "I am the Lord, and there is no other" (Isa. 45:18, NIV).

"Out of chaos God made a world, and out of high passions comes a people." Lord Byron

~PRAYER ~

Father, I look to You to thank You for what You have created in me, to conform me to the awesomeness of whom and what You say I am. You knew me before I knew myself; help me to see me as You do. In You, I am not a mess, but I am truly blessed. I am fiercely, uniquely, and wonderfully made. I think differently, and You call that beautiful. I see things a little askew, and You say that's fine. You have given me a lovely perspective of positivity and peace. Now, Papa, I ask that You bless me to see and to *love* others the way I am loved by You. Help me to show and share what so freely You have given me. Thank You, Papa, for Your Love! In Jesus's name, Amen.

~YOUR PRAYER OR THOUGHTS FOR TODAY ~

Mini Read 3

Sometimes I Get Mad at God
(Inspired by my past—yes, I have one)

Yes, I hate to admit it, but this is a true statement for me: sometimes I get mad at God. Some things came about in my life over the years, and I must tell you that I wasn't that happy about how they turned out. Now, of course, looking back I realize Papa God had a bigger plan. It would have been oh so nice if Papa God had clued me in on said plan. Now isn't that funny. Who am I that He has to be mindful of little ol' me?

I betcha if any one of us were to look back over our lives and were allowed to see the view from where our Heavenly Papa is, we'd probably pass out. If I knew then the steps I would have to go through to be where I am right now, I think I would have hidden under the covers in the rinky-dink old bed in my then-old apartment and stayed there. It was scary, and I couldn't understand why God didn't just go and make things work out for me right then and there. I tell you I was mad.

During that time, I was a bigger mess than I knew, but we now know God can work with our mess. Seems to me God kind of likes to use people who are somewhat messed up. You know, like Gideon, David, Sampson, me (ROTFL). Well, it's true. Because everyone has something they need to work on within themselves. Maybe you too?

Anywho, back to my current story. Well, there I was a mess. My children's father and I had just gotten a divorce, and now our children needed emotional healing. I felt abandoned, unattractive, useless, and worthless as a woman and as a mate. I felt unworthy, and I felt like giving up on everything and everyone. I am sure my children's father probably felt the same way, and for that, I am so very sorry. I never meant to hurt him; I didn't. I guess you can see why I was just a bit angry with God at that time. I couldn't understand why He allowed such horrendous things to happen in "my" life. What the hell! Because it felt like hell was what I was living. While writing this, I remember me back then, but it is not who I am today.

Still, there were times I prayed for God to come and get me, just take me home to heaven. I needed God to save me and felt like nothing was happening. There was no savior to rescue me; it seemed like no one, not even God, cared if I made it or not. I was pretty angry and scared. I spent a lot of time alone, lonely, broke, and emotionally destitute. I was pretty miffed. No, I wasn't; oh, heck, I was pissed off. I was getting pretty angry with—no, I was *mad* at God. And you know what? I told Him so!

Actually, I yelled at Him. I threw my Bible across the room like I could hurt God with it. Luckily (really, I wouldn't call it luck) I can say He didn't strike me down. He didn't cripple me or crush me. Here I sit writing to you now my story because of His love for me. Whew! I don't recommend doing it that way. But just in case you do, you can know that our God can deal with your anger or you being mad at Him. He was able to handle me and my stuff, and I'm sure He can handle you and whatever stuff you've got. Looking back on those days makes me kinda sad. Why didn't I just calm down, trust and listen to God? Honestly, I just was not able to at the time.

Thankfully God knew my heart deep down even when I didn't. I guess I needed to know I could be, and that I was, His daughter. I needed to be honest and tell Him how hurt I was. It was okay for me to ask Him where he was, if He had forgotten me, if He too had abandoned me. Could I really go to Him, and He would give me rest? 'Cause I was tired—really, really tired. Did God sincerely love me? I so desperately wanted someone to honestly (unconditionally) love me. I thought, Where the hell are you, God? Not in hell; He already won that battle. But still, during this time I was out of it, mad and angry with life and with God. Has anyone else ever been there? It's okay if you have, and it's all right if you are, because sometimes you just get mad at God. Go ahead tell Him; our Heavenly Father can handle it. He can deal with it. He's got you.

Well, let me share this with you: Those days are far behind me now. Thank you, God! Whew! It doesn't mean I don't have bad days anymore. Why? Because I now have a deeper relationship and constant communication with God. It doesn't mean I've got this thing called life all under control, because I don't just yet. What it means is I have come to trust Papa God, because He saw and sees the big picture of my life. From His vantage point, things are looking pretty good. You know what I'm saying to you is it's your turn now. Allow God into your heart. Share with Him your hurts, your joy, good days, and fun times too. Share your anger and your fears, and trust He will not leave you or abandon you. He loves and has blessings for you that you are not aware of yet. Trust in Him and His timing, and you won't have to be mad anymore.

~MEDITATION MOMENTS ~

My God, my God, why have you forsaken me? Why are you so far from saving me, from the words of my groaning? O my God, I cry by day, but you do not answer, and by night, but I find no rest. Yet you are holy, enthroned on the praises of Israel. In you our fathers trusted; they trusted, and you delivered them. To you they cried and were rescued; in you they trusted and were not put to shame (Ps. 22:1–5, ESV).

"For every minute you are angry, you lose sixty seconds of happiness." Ralph Waldo Emerson

"The truth will set you free, but first it will piss you off."
Gloria Steinem

~PRAYER ~

Heavenly Father, bless me to know that Your timing for my life is wonderful and preciously precise and perfect in every way that concerns me and mine. Bless me to know I can come to You openly and honestly and You still love me. You always have, and You always will. Bless me to know I don't have to wait until I am a ticking time bomb before I come to You. Help me to know I can come to You anytime, every time. You are a loving, kind, and generous Father, and You are mine, and I am *Yours*! I can trust You in all things and know You have heard me. You will answer with beautiful and good things. Thank You, Heavenly Father, for being so patient and good to me. Thank You even when the answer is no. Bless Your Holy Name! *Amen.*

~YOUR PRAYER OR THOUGHTS TODAY ~

Mini Read 4

God Is Watching!
(Inspired by Santa)

God is watching—not looking for who's naughty or nice like Santa Claus.

This is probably not for those of you who are honoring and serving an all-seeing, all-knowing, ever-present, everywhere, "I am" God! You may not need to be reminded of who He is; but just in case you forgot, meditate on this.

Did you know the standards the Lord put in place when Jesus was walking the earth are still relevant today? What I find, though (and this is probably only for me), is somehow it appears to get harder and harder to do and say the right things in everyday life situations. I believe there are some of you who are able to do and say the right things most of the time. Me personally, much to my regret, I fall short on many occasions. Pray for me as God continues to work in my life.

I have found that the same loving God who gave us His son Jesus is the same God who is in my corner when I sin, make a mistake, or just plain screw it all up. Do I do and say the right things? The answer for me is sometimes yes and sometimes no. Because sometimes I am just living selfishly—not caring about the consequences or how my actions or decisions affect anyone else. I just don't care. That's really sad.

By now you're wondering where does "God is watching" come in. Go ahead and ask Him, "Where are You, Papa God?" For those of you who are more formal with your heavenly Dad, "Where are You, Father"? Either way will work, as long as it is a question from your heart to Him. Well, did you ask Him?

There are so many times when I've just screwed it all up. I keep doing the same stupid thing over and over again. Not realizing at the moment that God has and will give me all that I need to overcome all the crap in my life. So when I flub it, He is there to pick me up and forgive me as many times as I can open my mouth to ask. Now I get it—there are consequences for my actions, good or bad. God is watching over me—not to condemn me or throw me under the bus, or to condone my destructive actions. But He is generously showing His love, mercy, and grace.

Allow me to share a story; yes, I'm taking a rabbit trail. I used to try and scare my children into doing the right thing by telling them God was always "watching," so they had better be good—sort of like a Santa Claus situation. That worked for about an hour. It was a type of manipulation and control, not cool or right. I later learned that it was better to teach them that when they are in a rough or challenging situation, the "Greater One" (God through the Holy Spirit) lives inside of them. I told them a loving God is always with them, "watching," waiting, and protecting them. I've tried to teach them that if they would just call out to God, He would graciously give them guidance to make the right choices. Even now that they are grown and out of college, I still remind them, and myself, that God the Father is always with us and "watching" over us now and eternally. This brings such peace to us, and it can for you too. Again, not a Santa Claus God but a loving Heavenly Father.

So now imagine God, the creator of the universe—no, the creator of everything—is watching you. He's not hating you but loving you. He's loving you through all your "boo-boos," your mistakes, your blowouts, and your blowups. Honestly so many of us are so busy believing God is looking for a reason to smash us to bits that we can't believe He really does love and care about our daily living. You see, God is in the business of giving us every opportunity to overcome our negative ways by giving us as many chances as we may need to do so. However, I'm not saying you get to go ahead and do whatever you want to do without any consequences, because, well, that's just not true. What I am saying is that God does not solely exist to condemn you of every mistake or sin you have committed. I believe if that were true, humanity would no longer exist.

God is a good Father, and He does not create mistakes, mishaps, uh-ohs, oopsies, or—excuse my language here—crap. You are none of the above, just so you know.

God is watching, but He is excited at the progress you have achieved and that you are about to achieve. It's like you're on a baseball field, and so far, each time at bat you've struck out (bad choices, bad timing). But today, unlike all the days before, you actually recognized that God is speaking to you. In your heart you hear, "You've got this. Just focus, and you can do it!" Something inside you leans into what you heard, and you grasp it. The pitcher and shortstop communicate, the pitcher is winding up, he aims that baseball for the outside corner because he has seen your weaknesses before. (Sounds like the enemy, right? He has seen your weaknesses before and attacks from that vantage point.) But yeah, this time you focus, and as the ball is coming across the corner of that plate, bam, there is a connection among you, the ball, the bat, and your inner strength (the Father's love inside you, the truth about how incredibly awesome you are) and you get a bona fide base hit. "Aw, man," you say, "but I didn't hit a home run." But Papa God is saying, "Did you see that hit [progress] they just did? That was awesome!" He is jumping up and down and, I imagine, being your greatest cheerleader! You make it to second base off that play, and one man runs in for a score! Wow, you connected; you did it! Then you say to yourself, "So Papa God, what else can I do with You watching over me?"

Now think about all the dreams, daydreams, and odd things you've been thinking about. Maybe now is the time to go ahead and give them a try! Our Father, who is in heaven, is there for us, no matter how many times we believe we have failed. I say try again—this time knowing God believes in you, that He always has and always will. And that thing you've been dealing with time and time again that has disrupted your life and torn your personal, private world apart again and again— know that our God is watching. Watching not to spank you or call you out, so to speak, but to call you *up*. You have everything you need to overcome whatever it is that holds you back and keeps you stuck. In God and with God and because our Heavenly Father, well, "He don't make no junk." You got this; now go get 'er done!

~MEDITATION MOMENTS ~

I will instruct you and teach you in the way you should go; I will counsel you with my loving eye on you (Ps. 32:8, NIV).

"Everything may not be OK, but if God is with you, you will be OK." Mark Driscoll

~PRAYER ~

Heavenly Papa, I am calling on You today to walk me through whatever I may encounter. Please continue to be with me and cause me, through Your goodness, to do the right things even when I think I'm gonna mess it all up again. Help me to see myself and all Your incredible creations through Your eyes. In this and everything You are to me and I am to you, I thank You, Lord! In the name of Your most holy son, Jesus Christ. *Amen.*

~YOUR PRAYER OR THOUGHTS FOR TODAY ~

Mini Read 5

What Would You Have Me Say, Father?
(Inspired by my need to justify myself)

Our real-life situations often offer opportunities for God to reveal to us the proper ways of dealing with unexpected and unwanted unpleasant and hurtful circumstances. The following story is the result of one of those times in my life.

The Lord had me write this letter to an associate of mine after this person had, in my opinion, wronged me once again. I desired to challenge them, but really, I was looking to vindicate myself. I wanted to make my point. I wanted that person to know that what they did hurt me to the core.

Even more than that, I wanted them to hurt like I was hurting. But I decided to take time to focus on the Lord. This is what I believe God gave me to express to them instead of what I really wanted to say, which would not have been good and would have made matters much worse. This is what I wrote:

"I pray that you are having a blessed day and week. I pray that the Father in heaven will answer all of your prayers and do so swiftly and promptly. I pray you have peace, love, and joy! I pray you have all that your heart desires, and that God adds to those desires ones you didn't even know you needed. I pray that for the rest of your life your walk with God the Father will be an ever-increasing and flourishing experience. I also pray that your every need is met by the Loving Creator Himself."

Love became the focus rather than my anger and pain. It was a viewpoint that changed my perception of the situation. It changed my heart, my words, and my mind. It was a response out of love, not a reaction out of pain. It was a gentle reminder to me of how God sees me when I say or do the wrong thing. It was seeing through the eyes of love.

Please know that at first, I felt like Jonah and the whale: "God, you have got to be kidding me." Why on earth would He have me say this! When He knew she was a sourpuss. It seemed to me that she was always trying to "put me in my place," and not a good place either. I felt I should have had the right to defend myself, to correct this matter as I saw fit. But once I made the decision to pray for God's direction and allow Him to vindicate me, there was a precious peace and feeling of love that arose within me, and I knew He was right.

Even when God showed me the right response, I still had to choose to say what I heard Him say to me in my heart. I had to choose to forgive her. I had to decide to do and say the right things. Knowing the right thing to do without choosing to do the right thing is absolutely pointless.

Like most people, my version of what happened seemed right. I'm sure that her side of the story seemed right to her too. Honestly, the most important side of every story is God's view of it.

God called me to be the bigger person, to show love and forgiveness. It felt better not to be a part of a painful mess. My heart was happy, and a smile came over my face as I realized

God in heaven would choose to use me in such a beautiful way. And you know what? I got released from anger and hurt. And best of all, our relationship was restored, and we now have a wonderful friendship at the time of this writing.

Now, you may have a similar situation you are facing or may face in the future. How will you handle it? What will be the outcome of your story? Will it end the way you want it to, where you justify yourself? Or will you choose God's story for you, where there is peace, love, and restoration? You get to choose!

~MEDITATION MOMENTS ~

Put on then, as God's chosen ones, holy and beloved, compassionate hearts, kindness, humility, meekness, and patience, 13 bearing with one another and, if one has a complaint against another, forgiving each other; as the Lord has forgiven you, so you also must forgive. 14 And above all these put on love, which binds everything together in perfect harmony. (Col. 3:12–14, ESV).

Let all bitterness and wrath and anger and clamor and slander be put away from you, along with all malice. 32 Be kind to one another, tenderhearted, forgiving one another, as God in Christ forgave you (Eph. 4:31–32, ESV).

"Forgiveness is an act of the will, and the will can function regardless of the temperature of the heart." Corrie Ten Boom

~PRAYER ~

Father, I look to You and ask You to guide me in every way. Holy Spirit, help me to pray what You would have me pray and say. I ask that You bless me to walk in unconditional love. Thank You for blessing me not to focus on the faults of others but to focus on the beauty You have formed within each of us. I ask to be blessed to live daily accepting the love You've given me and giving and sharing that love with others.

Thank you for leading me to bless rather than to be or start a mess. *Amen.*

Mini Read 5

~YOUR PRAYER OR THOUGHTS FOR TODAY ~

Mini Read 6

The "Ish" of Life
(Inspired by my nephew M. S. Jr.)

*M*y nephew shared this term with me through his Facebook page. How does one begin talking about the "ish" in your life? Actually, this is just another way to say the "crap" in your life. Okay, now that we have an understanding of what "ish" is, let's talk about it.

For some reason, folks don't think USNs—what I mean is Christians, true followers of Christ—have crap. You see, I am just an old Southern chick and a Sol Cal Southern gal, and that's just exactly how I think and talk inside my head and out loud. As you read on in this book, you might think I'm crazy; and I really am crazy—crazy for Jesus! I feel like this might give some of y'all some insight into how I view some things, help you guys stick with me here.

Well, let me tell you something, Christians are no different—are just pieces to out to shout. What? What am I saying? Yes? That's right, sometimes we have "ish" hit the fan. Sometimes we get sick, we get pissed off, cussed, job loss, large amounts of debt, house broken, and just plain old wacky things. We are just done just like everybody else. Well, we do! I read that somewhere—oh yeah, it's in the Bible. Plus we know if we keeping marching forward, things work together for us as we keep our focus on the One. While we are trying to look to Him, for Him, it can get unhinged sometimes.

If you're a brand-new Christian and you think all is hunky-dory now, on the one hand you're right; but on the other hand, there is a good chance you could be challenged in some area of your life. Probably where you are already the weakest! Oh, honey, baby child, let me tell ya. I have some really "good news" for you, though. You have everything you already need to beat, resist, and overcome whatever is coming at you or that's coming your way.

Yeah, that's right, becoming an USN is like being in the best, most exclusive (and inclusive) club ever in all of heaven and on earth. By the way, it's free to join. It will cost you nothing, but you will gain total freedom and liberty, and all your needs will be met. We can show you how. All you have to do is be all that you were created to be—God's "original intent" for you. Your becoming one of the USNs is vital, because as someone once taught me, "to resist is futile" (bah wah ha ha ha!).

No, really, whether you do or don't, the good news is still gonna get ya.

What does all of this have to do with the "ish"? Well hang on; I am about to share that with you right now. What it boils down to is this: when our "poo" hits the proverbial fan, and it does from time to time, we run to our source—our Papa God! When one of us USNs gets cancer, we turn to the one who has the answer. Papa God is our provider, our source for every hindrance that could come along. Now sometimes that may mean we have to get that surgery, and sometimes it is actually miraculously healed! Oh, yeah, that's how good God is! I know some of you are asking, "Well, why did cancer or the bad thing happen in the first place?" You know we just don't have all the answers.

And some things happen to us because we are hardheaded, myself included. You know that funny feeling you get—that knowing in your heart that says, "Don't do it, bro; don't go there"? But of course, many of us do anyway. I believe that is God speaking to you, differentiating right from wrong, safety from harm. But again there we go anyway, and after we do, we are wallowing in the "ish" of the circumstances we created. Sound familiar? Well, we get to make a choice of doing what we know is right or being stubborn and doing our own thing. But keep in mind there could be consequences; there are almost always consequences, whether seen or unseen.

Well, it may come down to choices. Darn it, I hate choices. I can't stand that word sometimes. It feels like a four-letter word to me of the worst kind—*choice*! Why can't Papa just make me do the right thing? Why doesn't He just make me a robot and make me listen? Why doesn't He just stop the bad guys from causing harm? He doesn't because our Father in heaven is a gentle Man, and He gives everyone the power to choose—a choice to do the right thing or the mean and evil thing. He needs your coming to Him to be a decision, a choice that you make, not a forced or manipulated or falsely engineered event!

I tell you Papa God is so wonderful; He will meet you right where you are. This is so easy. It's like opening a gift on Christmas morning, every morning! You get to know who you are and *whose* you are. You get to live in a lifestyle that "rocks." You get to walk in more than enough of every good thing you'll ever need. And the most important thing is that you get to overcome the "ish" of life in and through *Him*.

~MEDITATION MOMENTS ~

Blessed is the one who perseveres under trial because, having stood the test, that person will receive the crown that the life Lord has promised to those who love him (James 1:12, NIV).

And we know that for those who love God all things work together for good, for those who are called according to his purpose. (Rom. 8:28, ESV).

"As long as we remain in the body we shall be subject to a certain amount of that common suffering which we must share with all the sons of men." A. W. Tozer

~PRAYER ~

Father God, You are so good! No matter what, I am so thankful You are always there. No matter how far away from You I feel, You are always there; You never leave me. I am thankful and grateful that when life seems to be at its worst in my eyes, You, Heavenly Father, are more than able to handle on my behalf the junky stuff, the bad things, the ill health, the financial woes, and the hard times that come. I understand that bad times come no matter what, but I thank You for blessing me to come knowing that You are there to take me by the hand and walk me through to "Victory"! When I get scared, and I do from time to time, You are the person and the place I can and will run to. When the "ish" hits the fan, I know inside myself that You didn't leave me to fend for myself alone and lonely; You are always here to walk me through. I am asking now, Father, help me in my time of need so that I may thank You and continue to thank You in my time of plenty and successes! To shout, "The world my God is Lord, and through Him all good and wonderful things are possible, even overcoming the 'ish' in my life!" Amen.

~YOUR PRAYER OR THOUGHTS FOR TODAY ~

Mini Read 7

**When It Hurts, Cry;
But Cry Out To GOD!**

(Inspired by a close family going through a difficult time)

What does one say when there is death, when there is betrayal, when there is disappointment? How do you react to the big C (cancer)? What do you do when fear comes upon you in the middle of the night? Of course, your faith steps in and you pray, right? That would be good, but sometimes you just have to cry.

Yes, I mean have a good, old-fashioned cry. But while you are crying, cry out to the Lord. He's already there waiting to hold you in His arms the way a good father should. He's cradling your head right at those moments when the pain is just too much to bear on your own. Some of you have desperately wondered how you made it through the night. You know that night when you cried so hard your eyes felt like they would just close shut. I tell you it wasn't because you're so strong on your own; whether you recognized it or not, it was Papa God who got you through. Some of you think, "Well, I am not a Christian or a believer." That's okay, because Papa God believes in you. Like any "good father," whether you are doing everything He has asked you to or not, He is still your "Father." What this means is that in the midst of your tears, your sorrows, your pain, or your loss, He is right there beside you holding you up and sometimes carrying you when you can't handle it anymore. He is just waiting for you to recall that night (asking, "Why, God? Why me, why this, why now?"—but then that's another story) when you felt a precious and sweet presence and dismissed it, when you swore you heard a voice from outside of yourself but also from within saying, "I promise you tomorrow will be a better day," and lo and behold it was and still is.

So I cried, cried, and cried, and even though I knew the Father's love and His touch, His voice, I still cried. I was scared and afraid, so I would have to put my hope and trust in the Lord, because I knew He had me. Some believe because we know Him that we don't get afraid or scared, or fall or become the fallen, or make horrifically bad mistakes and judgment calls. Well, I have news for you pre-Cs (pre-Christians), and maybe even for some of you "religious" folks and some Christians. And please understand that religion and Christianity are not necessarily the same: The first is mostly a bunch of rules and severe structure, where the second one is about a relationship with the One that we are to walk out daily. Yes, there is direction, and a confirmed framework to follow, but practiced out of love, honor, and respect, not punishment. We are yet to be perfected or perfect in any way. This is why we call on our Heavenly Father, because we wonder without His steady hand in our lives and world how on earth we would make it without Him. Newsflash, we would not and could not hold up to this life we live without Him.

I can just see His ageless and strong hand reaching over and wiping tears away, counting every one of them as He places them in the bottle(s) marked with our names on them. Holding us close the way a mother does when her baby is crying (when her baby is now twenty-five instead of five) and they don't make a Band-Aid big enough for the hurting heart. But God does! So she wishes she could just absorb all of her child's hurts and pains and wash them all away. The "good news" is that where she cannot, our Papa God can, and He does just that. He is the Band-Aid; He is the salve for the wounds that you feel will never be able to be healed or go away.

So you cry and cry and cry some more. I know it hurts, and for that I am so very sorry; but I have a response. It's not that I can make anything stop hurting, but please allow me to introduce you to the one who can. "God's able" sounds like something a little ol' grandma would say, or perhaps one of these kind and loving, cheesy Christians today, right? I tell you this: I know it is true! Because both describe me.

I ask that you put God to the test. He can, He will, and yes, He wants to help! Allow Papa God to reach out to you in the midst of your tears. No matter what the situation or circumstance are, allow Him access, and you'll not be sorry. I use the word *allow* because our Heavenly Father is a "gentleman" in every sense of the word. Know this: He will never force Himself or His will upon you, but as you invite Him into your world. For some of us it will be p-i-e-c-e by piece, but then in doing so your p-e-a-c-e will come. He will walk you through and show you some wonderful things about yourself, some things that will need to be cleared out and cleaned up, and you'll never feel condemned, but you will know correction. Correction is not rejection; when done properly, it is just another form of love.

So the next time it hurts, and you don't know what else to do, I say go ahead and cry, but while you're crying, cry out to God! He's already there, ready to wipe your tears and see you through. God has and is your answer!

~MEDITATION MOMENTS ~

This poor man cried, and the Lord heard him and saved him out of all his troubles. (Ps. 34:6, ESV).

Then they cried to the Lord in their trouble, and he delivered them from their distress. (Ps. 107:6, ESV).

"Listen to God with a broken heart. He is not only the doctor who mends it, but also the father who wipes away the tears." Criss Jami

~PRAYER ~

Father, Your word clearly tells me there will be troubles, fear, and sadness to come into our lives from time to time, but Your word also says when I am scared, You've got me. That you are the lifter of my head. That though I walk through a deep and dark place, and it seems that death is all around, I need not be afraid because you are with me! I choose to call on your name, Heavenly Father, to dry my tears, to quiet myself so that I may hear your voice for guidance and direction. I will lean on you for my peace, my comfort, and allow you access to my heart, my soul, my mind, and my body to bring what only you can, the way only you can. Yes, Heavenly Father, I will allow you to dry my tears, teach me to bless those who may have hurt me in the process. And I now say, to God be all the glory; in the name of Jesus, *amen*!

~YOUR PRAYER OR THOUGHTS FOR TODAY ~

Mini Read 8

Sticks and Stones
(Inspired by redirection for my life from God)

I would like to share this MINI because this one is dear to me. I've come to know and believe that things—good things or bad things or even the unjust things that happen—affect us in one way or another. Well, sometimes we wonder where "God" is in all of this, especially in the injustices that happen. We wonder why He allows bad things to happen to such good people. How could this be? I would like to share one of my own stories based on what seemed unjust and unfair to me at the time. And I think I'm a good person too. Hopefully my story will help someone else see that there is a silver lining after all. That maybe, just maybe, Papa God was there all along. That's how I made it through; that's why I'm still standing—a little shaky, a little sore, a little scared. But then, no one ever died from being shaky or a little scared, so here goes.

You know the adage "Sticks and stones may break my bones, but words will never hurt me"? Well, I believe it's a lie from the pit of hell itself. At least for me, words at different times and stages of my life have just about destroyed me. I say this because we must keep in mind the power of words in our lives. The words we use create a negative or positive atmosphere. When we speak or write mean, hurtful words, they can destroy the individual they are aimed at. Have you ever received a compliment? I am sure you have, and do you remember how good that felt? Well, our mean, destructive words do the exact opposite. You see, I now have a new adage: "Sticks and stones may break my bones, but those damn mean words can just about kill me." But that was because I was focusing on the words of people and not on what my Heavenly Papa was and is saying about me. Honestly, before you read on, keep this in mind: if we reflect God's goodness, then we must be "flippin' fly" (that means we are incredibly awesome, terrifically wonderfully, and absolutely amazing). Now on to my story.

You see, before Papa could get my attention to teach me how to dream again and to take time to rest and be creative, I got broadsided. I got the hell knocked out of me. Because I was so focused on trying to be a successful professional that I at times neglected other important parts of my life, including and especially myself. I say this because although we are to think of others first, I've learned to first love myself. Because without that, it is impossible to love, care, or think well of others. Because if you can't love the creation of *you* that God made, how can you possibly love, care about, bless, or even like anyone else? You see, I realize now that the events that were supposed to encourage me to dream and be creative unfortunately got usurped by the enemy, who in so many ways was able to discourage me from doing what I'm doing right now: sharing my stories. You see, the adversary, the enemy" the devil—oh, shoot, let's just call him what he is: a poo-head—often uses our God-given talents and abilities to destroy us.

I realize that my ability to share the heart of our Heavenly Father, to allow myself to come alongside of God and share how He expresses Himself to me and then through me to others is a precious gift. God chooses to use us all to some degree or another by allowing us to participate in His grand plan for us, for humanity. He enjoys giving us a choice and an opportunity to be or play a positive role in someone else's life. When how He created us and how we choose to live and function connects with His goodness, it just makes everything even better. The reason for my personal hesitation was because I was too afraid to trust the words I was hearing Papa God speak to me. He had been speaking to me all along; I know this now. I can step back now and recognize how the enemy was trying to use *words* against me to try to stop me. What could the enemy be doing to try to stop you?

Okay, back to my story about the poo-head and what he tried to do. I was "encouraged" to leave said place of employment of nineteen years, which was such a sad, awkward, painful, and devastating time in my life. You see, I started at ground level, and through diligence, dedication, and hard work, I was promoted numerous times all the way up to senior management. Oh, but then I got taken down a few notches. After having worked so hard to get to one of the top positions of that company, they came at me, y'all. It no longer mattered how much money the company itself poured into my advancement (by the way, thousands and thousands of dollars). They educated me well in more ways than one. They educated me in the art of backstabbing, how to climb the proverbial corporate ladder, and how to finagle the truth. Yes, I did walk away with some excellent management skills, but that was quite an education and a very good one at that. Girl, they didn't even care.

I always felt out of sorts, out of place, just not quite prepared. You know, like I didn't quite belong. Ever felt that way in life? There is a reason for that. For me, my beginnings at the company didn't allow me some of the accesses one of my counterparts had. She was becoming one of the best that company ever saw or would see. She had maintained her integrity and excellent character along the way as well. That being said, she was groomed for success within the company, where I was sort of exposed to it. I tell you it is not the same, where she was immersed in the company, "drenched" with inside knowledge, I got "drizzled." I was like the caramel drizzle on the top of your latte, while she got mixed in with the latte itself—very different. Don't mind me, honey, as I am venting here as well. I'm just trying to let it all go. Come on with me now.

A long story short: I got into trouble when things started getting rough for my amazing and wonderful husband and me at home. We had so many issues going on, including my health; things were scary like for many of you out there. We almost lost our home, I got sick, and then I had to have surgery. We had one thing after another happening to us and our friends and family seemingly all at once. There appeared to be no mercy for me at work and no letup of the catastrophes happening at home.

With all the "ish" that was happening, I could not keep up with my professional responsibilities—I dropped the ball. I guess that was my very own fault, and although I cried out for help, that help came all too late. With management, it was all about the numbers, and my numbers were shot and I was at the bottom. Despite everything that was going on, I finally redeemed myself and my numbers before I was asked to step down. My final numbers were kick ass, just sayin'.

Unfortunately, by that time it was already too late. In their eyes, I had failed, and the result was a horrific performance review. The very words that were written about me almost destroyed me and my confidence in every area of my life. I don't know if I can convey the devastation I felt. The agony, degradation, and inhumanity of it all were painfully overwhelming. Please, everyone, please keep that in mind when writing mean things. Written words are just as hurtful and destructive as opening your mouth to speak them. It makes me sad that some people think they have the right to destroy another person's image and dignity. It hurts when folks are doing that.

I must say except for the love of God Almighty, who is *love*, my incredible husband's love and prayers, and the love and support from my true friends and family, I would have wasted away to nothing and reveled in it. All because of *words*! Those words went to the very core and essence of who I was at that time. I wanted to die and cease to exist—once again, all because of *words*! Written words that were harsh and cutting, spoken cruel words that bit like piranhas over and over on me and my life, about "mistakes" I had made, as if no one else ever made one. I say to you be careful, especially if you live in a glass house; you know what I mean. No one—I mean not one person—stepped in to console or defend me. No one stood up for the person many of them truly knew me to be. I stood alone in that place, or so I thought. All the while Papa God was setting a different stage for me—one that I would not be aware of for a little while yet. He allowed me to wallow in my sadness, bathe in my disappointments, and drink of the disillusionment of a weary mankind. My heart broke into a million pieces. It seriously shattered my faith, and so I began to question it. Have you ever experienced such heartache, such pain? Oh, but look at us now. We are still here all because of God and His mercy, grace, and amazing love.

After what was done to me, I felt incapable of even being a "normal human being." What was written and conveyed about me was so depressing and demeaning, I wondered who would ever want me to do anything ever again. Who would want me as an employee; better yet, who could value me as viable person? Did it matter if I even had a pulse? After that, I started to believe I was incapable of doing anything worthwhile. It was debilitating to my spirit, to my soul, and to my body. I felt defeated and became depressed, and for a moment I wore the "victim mentality" because of those damning *words*. I tried to recover but could not muster up the energy to believe in myself again. I kept on reading them over and over again, allowing them to sink in to every fiber of my petty little existence. I let someone else's view of myself to determine my life's direction and destiny. In those moments, their words had more value to my life than God's! I was ready to shut it all down. I almost threw in the towel, but God—thank God for being God—He would not allow me to stay in that place. He is such a good God, a loving and kind Father; He could not, would not, and did not let me down.

For the record, that was not the first time in my life something like that had happened to me (sounding familiar to anyone?). In my first marriage, which was not successful, we each used *words* of destruction to demolish the other. We sank to lows that two people who took vows to honor and love each other through all the troubles of the world should never have experienced. The truth is we were just growing and becoming discontent with each other, but it wasn't how either of us thought it would be. Our maturation didn't appear like we envisioned. We were becoming and growing as individuals, but we were not becoming and growing as a corporate family. I am sorry to admit this, but at the time, I had not grown in my walk with Papa God to a place of maturity of any kind I felt at this time. And by the way, I'm still growing. I can only speak for myself in this. I was just awful, but as my pastor taught us, "Hurt people, hurt people." This is not an excuse but a fact. Fortunately, and thankfully, I had the good sense to spare my children from the despicable things I was speaking about their dad. Somehow, I had the wisdom to know when and to whom to speak such atrocities and did not speak about those things in front of the kids or to them. I believe those words could have backfired and destroyed their view of me and not so much of the other parent.

Many years ago, I was one of the worship leaders at the church I was attending at the time. During this time, I made a terrible, horrific, and stupid choice, and it cost me. It caused me to have to give up my ministry for some time—a ministry I loved and still love. It cost me relationships I had cultivated for years. It cost me a part of me. I was approached by a few folks with *words* that would have led to my demise if God had not been there to hold me up. Only this time I wanted to die. I mean I wanted to physically die because of the horrible things people felt they had the right to say to me and about me. Once again, people found new and inventive ways to use the English language for destruction and humiliation. I already knew what I had done, but what I needed would be hard to come by. I needed love, compassion, support, and forgiveness—not for what I had done wrong but to help me come back from my error in judgment and my mistake. Sometimes we church folk are the cruelest of them all, and I have lived both sides of that,

I am sad to say. I am grateful for my pastors who did justly by me, scooped me up and loved me through it all. Thank God they never gave up on me. Also, they did not spare the spiritual rod, so to speak, but all of it was done in love, so I never felt less than anyone else in their lives. Thank You for being such a wonderful example of our "Savior and King" and using *words* to encourage and build. You built me back up with God's *words*. I desire to do the same for someone else if I ever get an opportunity to.

We all know bad things can and do happen to good people. We don't always have the answers to why. Sometimes it's us; we make dumb choices of our own. Some people want to blame someone else no matter what. They don't want to look in the mirror and take responsibility for their own choices and actions. I know for a fact at times in my life I've done just that, even when my actions have affected someone else's life. Because they always do, be it in a good or bad way. But I am thrilled to tell you this much: God stepped in and rescued me from myself. I know He loves me and still sees me as valuable, still sees something good in me, and still sees the worth of His creation. How wonderfully awesome! Yes, with all the mistakes and bad choices I have made, I still consider myself a "pretty good" person because God does too. He believes I am worth it and worth it all. Heavenly Papa sees you the same way too, you know. You're worth it too. I realize some people can't see anything good in us, and that's their perspective, their view. So we will just have to be okay with that. You and I may never convince some of those folks otherwise, but sweetheart, life goes on. We can live a good life despite them and/or their views. Because the only words that should matter, the only words we should be giving credence to, are the words of our

Heavenly Papa. He says only good things about us and to us. He speaks love and healing and gives us grace and mercy. His words bring us to life and heal everything the world has broken in us, whether because of our bad choices or the decisions of others. Always remember this: God's word rules.

So where am I going with this? Here is the point I am trying to make:. Our Heavenly Papa sees the good in us. He only says good things about us and only speaks good things to us, for that matter. He believes in His creation. That is you and me, by the way—not just nature, not just the great big vast universe, but us; we are His creation, just sayin'. I tell you what: that makes me happy and fills my life with excitement and joy. Don't you get it? Some of us keep going around saying, "There must be more than this?" If we could just understand what His beautiful words are saying about us, we would know that the last statement I made is true. There is so much more than this! I was created beautifully. I was made for something wonderful. This means and absolutely includes *you* too!

Heavenly Father is so good. He isn't trying to destroy you, but instead He wants to build you up. Ask yourself this: "What good, loving dad goes around destroying his own family or home?" Well, I believe a good dad would not do that. A good dad would love his family, give loving words of direction, build up his sons, encourage his daughters, and love and honor his wife. He would use encouraging words to build up his home, community, and workplace. My goodness, who wouldn't want to be in that family and have that dad? You are crazy if you don't! Why, because then Mom is empowered with the kind, loving words coming from her husband. He calls her lover, mother, friend, and confidant—all she is meant to be. Because of this, their children can grow up with values and know self-worth by the words and actions of their parents. You see, you all rock and give so much more than you know as you imitate our Heavenly Father and His words.

That being said, if a mere man can do these things, how much more, then, will the Creator of everything good and wonderful do for you? Before you were even born, God had great plans for you. He spoke and speaks only good things over you. Papa God has spoken words to bring prosperity, words to bring health, words to empower you. Words that speak life and bring joy. Words to make one reflect on who they are and think about those things that are good and uplifting. Words that are promising and positive.

You see, words are powerful; they give life or death to a situation. Ever been somewhere and one insensitive individual says one wrong thing and it completely changes the atmosphere? Well, that is what the enemy does. Have you ever been around someone who is always positive, always has positive things to say no matter the situation? Now that's walking with Papa God. I say, "Look out for the beautiful things God says about you, about your today and all of your tomorrows." It is pretty flippin' good. I don't know about you, but I would rather accept Papa God's words about me than some of the miserable things I think and speak over myself.

Well, back to said employer and my awful written review. I can now say with confidence that that is where I was supposed to be at the time. All has not been revealed to me just yet. I can sincerely speak blessings, though, to them and now walk in the peace and joy my Heavenly Papa always intended for me. Their words no longer will be legitimized in my life or my world, for that matter. I thank God for what I learned from them. I can give respect to a people that didn't and don't seem to warrant it, because of a creative miracle in my heart. That's where I am now. How about you? Got any stuff or situations, people, you need to let go of? Putting them in God's hands is so much better. I say do it; say these things out loud and watch what your own kind words will do. Remember the freedom of forgiveness!

Because of the Creator's love and rescue of me, I am now doing what I love doing: writing! I wonder if I had been able to stay at that company, would I have given myself the room to hear the direction or redirection I know I got from God? To hear His heart and follow *Him*? Funny thing: my mother reminded me that "writing" ridiculous stories or being able to put down in words my feelings and my thoughts is my first love. Well, actually Papa God is my first love, but you know what I mean. And from this moment forward, I hope that for you, like the day I got my epiphany, my revelation of my redirection, the only words that will matter most in my life are *His*, my Heavenly Father's! Now Your turn!

~MEDITATION MOMENTS ~

Do not let any unwholesome talk come out of your mouths, but only what is helpful for building others up according to their needs, that it may benefit those who listen. 30 And do not grieve the Holy Spirit of God, with whom you were sealed for the day of redemption. (Eph. 4:29-30, NIV).

"Kind words can be short and easy to speak, but their echoes are truly endless." Mother Teresa

"Think twice before you speak, because your words and influence will plant the seed of either success or failure in the mind of another." Napoleon Hill

~PRAYER ~

Heavenly Papa, You have given me an opportunity to speak life and blessings in a place that might have an unhealthy atmosphere. I say through You, Heavenly Papa, fill this place with Your goodness, give this place success, and bless everyone who walks through these doors. Give peace, wisdom, and clarity with vision to all You have called to lead in this place. Give all of us Your desire to honor and respect one another in the workplace, no matter our position, and in our homes and in this incredible world we live in. May in this day and all the days to come we live our lives to the full extent of greatness You have placed in us all. May our words be like Yours and bring life—not pain, nor sorrow, nor tears, nor sadness. I ask that You bless my words to bring confidence, peace, and love to a world so desperately in need of what You mean for all of us to have! *Your love unconditionally!*

Mini Read 8

~YOUR PRAYER OR THOUGHTS FOR TODAY ~

Mini Read 9

Supernatural Expectations
(Inspired by an actual event in my home!)

I had to have my appendix removed a few years back, and during my time of recuperation and healing, we had a visitor come and spend some time with us on the Sunday following my surgery.

It was abnormally quiet in our home that day as my beautiful grandchildren and their parents opted to allow "Noni" (that's me) time to rest and recover, so no visit from them that Sunday. As I stated, we had a visitor, and not a usual one at that. One of the young men who is like a son to me came over to spend some time with the family. Honestly, I think he was reassuring himself that I really was going to be okay.

He shared a wonderful experience he had during praise and worship at church that day. I hope one day he will share his story with others, as it still burns with great joy in my heart and mind. He said he could sincerely feel a tingling in his body, an experience he hoped would happen again. I wished I had been with him in that worship experience too. As the afternoon went on, we began sharing about the supernatural moves of

God, our expectations of God, and how He does them. To me, it seems God rarely answers us the way we think He should, could, or might. "Seriously, Heavenly Father, what the what?"

As we talked about the possibilities of how God has healed and moved in peoples' lives, even at that moment, I was personally trying not to have my own preconceived notions and expectations of God. Although I wondered how the Creator would, in fact, make me "whole again."

Relevant side note: Not only did the surgeon take my appendix, the polyp, and the growth attached to it, he also took out a small suspicious portion of my bowel to confirm there was no cancer. TMI much, I know.

I know sometimes as Christians, we use what I term "Christianese"—a whole other language almost, such as "whole again." If you are a baby Christian, or a pre-C as I call you (you know who you are), you may require some help navigating through the maze of Christian terms. Even now, from time to time, I get that look on my face, like, "What did you just say, and what the heck does that mean?" Anywho, back to my original "relevant side note." I'm happy to report that the doctor did not see a need to continue to take further random samples of my body and saw no need for possible reconstructive surgery. Whew! Thank you, Lord God above; hallelujah and amen (so be it—here I go again with more Christianese). Now, let's get back to sharing the story, shall we?

While my wonderful husband was making dinner (he's an excellent cook), our guest, my daughter, and I were sitting at the kitchen table. She was in college at the time, and we were surrounded by her math and accounting books, with calculators and pencils meticulously laid out. So you see the picture of the crowed table, which also had other essentials she felt necessary for preparation for her finals.

My son was upstairs doing what appeared to be hibernation. You know how teens can disappear for hours on end inside your own home. It seems that's what teens do, as he was about nineteen at the time. I believe they have done this since the dawn of teens; I'm sure of it, because that young man would rarely join the family downstairs. Teens, yeesh. He too was studying for finals and finishing things up to prepare for the end of the semester. And oh, they both aced their exams. Proud mama moment.

You probably have some sort of scene pictured in your mind right about now; if not, let me assist you. Three people sitting around a round glass table with metal legs, with books, medications, a couple of water bottles (or "clear liquid" if you are my spiritual son), some juice, and other misplaced items on top of it. The way the room is set up, if you are standing in the doorway to that section of the house, to your left is the kitchen, with a large island. The middle section of the area is the eat-in kitchen, with the sliding glass doors to the outside. Finally, the family room is to your right. Why am I sharing all of this with you? Because the backstory sets the scene for the "supernatural" God experience and expectation that was about to occur.

Our guest said to my daughter and me, "I'm thirsty." My daughter and I just looked at him in a way that said something like, "Then you had better do something about that, good buddy." Just a little smarty-pants attitude from both of us. Remember, my daughter had a stack of books in front of her, and I had been out of surgery and home from the hospital for maybe three to four days, so I was not moving so fast.

Then this young man, being the faith-filled person that he was, just stuck out his hand in anticipation that God would get him some water, or more like a scene straight out of *Star Wars*.

At this point, not a word was being spoken by my daughter and me. We stopped talking and began to look at him—not like he was crazy but like, "Okay, Lord, do your thing and make this happen for him." Basically, we joined our faith with his at that moment. You see, I believe I can fly, meaning I believe in the impossible. I believed my guest could fly too. And no, we are not being flippant or dishonoring our Lord. I know God can cure cancer, and I know he is able to provide a drink for a thirsty visitor.

As my guest reached for the bottle of water that was on the edge of the kitchen island, his eyes were still closed with anticipation and hope because he believed, trusted in, and had faith that could not be shaken as he had personally, tangibly experienced in the worship service that very day. He just knew God would somehow place the bottle into his hand. Not one word was spoken by anyone in that room; we could feel the profound, tangible presence of God in the house. This young man's faith was so real, so pure; he just knew after the experience he'd had during the praise and worship service that all things are possible. By now, the only sounds heard were some bustling here and there in the kitchen as my husband, or Papa as the kids call him, was still preparing dinner.

Oh, but then something wonderful happened. While this young man was sitting there, eyes closed, hand extended, he was ready to receive. His expectation was high, and like a ninja in a Bruce Lee movie, God did something unexpectedly awesome. The bottle floated across the room and landed in the young man's hand! At this point, my daughter and I were speechless. You would have been too!

Okay, okay, are you all ready for this?

So now that you've recovered your jaw, here's what actually had happened. The ninja, as we call my son, got the unction—meaning he felt or sensed the urge (more Christianese) to come downstairs to check to see what was going on. He was silent, and initially no one saw him enter the room, as is customary for ninjas. Keep in mind, all of this was taking place within about twenty to thirty seconds. My son stopped and looked in the room, and he saw our guest's hand extended toward the water. Then our son grabbed the water bottle from the counter, made motions to mimic the appearance of it floating in the air toward our guest, and gently placed it in his hand.

Of course, my daughter and I got to watch this whole event take place. It was sad, though, to see the total disappointment on the young visitor's face when he opened his eyes to see what had really happened. My son was so pleased to have helped his spiritual big brother that he did not quite understand the commotion of disappointment from our guest and the laughter coming from his sister and me. Papa was so immersed in dinner that he unfortunately never saw anything or was aware of what was going on.

Another relevant side note: I'm mentioning this because although Papa was there, he was completely unaware of what was taking place around him. So many of us have missed out on participating in something awesome because we are so busy with life. And although he was preparing dinner for us (really for me, as I was still recuperating), he did not get to be a part of the miraculous event that had just taken place in our home. Mary and Martha anyone? (More Christianese—Mary and Martha comprise a cool Bible story.) Not a bad thing but one could miss the "God thing" that could be going on around you. But being unaware—well, that's another story.

Immediately after all the commotion happened, I found myself speaking these words, and I knew then, like I do now, that this was God giving me the understanding to share with them a different perspective. I said:

"Son, you never told the Lord how you wanted the water bottle placed in your hand. I'm sure you envisioned it, though. You extended your hand in faith, believing, and somehow you knew God Almighty would make it happen. Now, why are you disappointed God didn't do it the supernatural way you expected or envisioned He would? What expectations did you place on God for your supernatural experience with Him to be?

"My son was not anywhere around when this event started, but for some reason, I believe the Lord called him down here to do this very act on His behalf. You see, sometimes God uses ordinary people to do extraordinary things. And sometimes He uses ordinary situations to produce supernatural results. My son grabbing the water bottle from the counter was an everyday, ordinary act. But placing it in your hands at that particular moment produced for you a supernatural result. Just because this event didn't happen the way you imagined it, and because God didn't do things the way you expected, do not discount the act or the person the Lord chose to use. God doesn't view life the way we do, because His ways are higher, meaning above whatever you can think of or dream of or envision. Even this I share with you now is just a minuscule view of our good Father's insight."

Basically, what I am asking is, "How many of us have prayed for supernatural intervention?" We all do and don't even realize that we have done just that. That being said, sometimes, not always, when the Creator chooses to send someone you know or use some average Joe to do what seems to be basic to answer or complete the request on your behalf, we discount the supernatural altogether because it just seems too simple to be God.

Now, I am not saying God doesn't do supernatural things. To the contrary, I am telling you from my personal life experiences. I believe, and I know, He still heals cancer and diabetes, and restores sight to the blind, physically and spiritually. He provides finances in times of need. *God still does miracles!* Got it?

~MEDITATION MOMENTS

Now to him who is able to do far more abundantly than all we ask or think, according to the power at work within us (Eph. 3:20, ESV).

"If you're going to have faith, you can't just have it when the miracles happen. You have to have it when they don't." Layla Rourke

"Miracles happen every day. Change your perception of what a miracle is and you'll see them all around you." Jon Bon Jovi

~PRAYER ~

Heavenly Father, help me to see the ways I have discounted the supernatural whether through a person or through my disbelief. At times I have doubted Your love for me and Your willingness to answer prayers on my behalf. I pray for wisdom in seeing things differently as You allow me to grow and become more like Your Son, Jesus. Bless me to stop putting You, my Lord, in a box even—and especially—when expecting those supernatural "miracles" I may so desperately need in my very own life and the lives of those I love.

Mini Read 9

~YOUR PRAYER OR THOUGHTS FOR TODAY ~

Mini Read 10

The God We Created
(Inspired by a deep discussion with my daughter J.)

Sometimes it seems we need God to validate us and our point of view because, of course, Heavenly Papa thinks just like us, right (ROTFL)? Well, doesn't he? This has been especially true for me when I've been in the midst of situations where I've felt trapped, infringed upon, or wronged. This MINI is about how we make God fit into our own personal boxes. By the way, God doesn't do boxes. We do, though. How?

By limiting Him in what we want Him to do for us instead of allowing Him to accomplish what he has planned for us USNs. When our lives are not working out like we think they should, that's when so many of us turn away from our Heavenly Father, because when we get mad, we get mad because God is not doing what we told Him to do!

Oh, and by the way, some of us call that prayer. I'm just saying! This MINI is also about those things in our lives that we have made our idols instead of God. It seems that from time to time, as I've done what I believed I was anointed—not just gifted or talented—to do, I looked for approval from a person or group of people, even though I was following what I heard Father God telling me to do. In those times, unfortunately, I don't recall seeking the Lord at all.

Please pray for me; as you can see, I need it. I sought certain people's approval of me, and here is the sad thing: they never did. Instead of being grounded in the Heavenly Father, I idolized a person's opinion of me or their assessments of my gifts, talents, and anointing. Because I admired them and what they had accomplished in their own lives, I sought their pat on my head as if I were that person's son or daughter, or even their dog in my case. Why wasn't I looking to my Papa God? Silly girl—silly, silly girl. All the while, I was not looking to the Creator for His love or guidance, or for His voice not even using His word. Instead, I incessantly looked to man, as in "mankind," for my "stamp of approval." Can you believe it? Yes, but God has been correcting that in me. Remember, I'm still a "mess in progress."

Don't judge; it can happen to anybody, even those of us who call ourselves Christians. Throughout my life, I realize that I have allowed different things and/or people, including my children, to become more significant than—and somehow more important to me than—God, just sayin'. It seems the everyday stuff we dabble in gets ahold of us and seems to take on a mind of its own and grabs our hearts and takes control of whatever is going on at that moment in time. You lose it, and life seems completely out of control, but there is always hope, but then that's another story.

You might use food, gambling, cigarettes, sex, alcohol, or the drug of your choice these days as your idol. Some make their clothes, their work, their social media status, or their bodies their idols. Some use their cars, their address, or their lifestyle as their God. It could be your favorite sports team—and oh, by the way, how come some of y'all scream, jump, and shout at the game and at the TV but worry about who might see you singing a song and praising God in church? Just a little beef of mine. This may sound mean, but for some of us, even their "sickness" becomes their God, and for others, their poverty is their God. Some people make themselves their own God. These days social media, and posting a selfie every hour, has fast become a god for some. Please know that our God—who created the universe, things big and small—wants to be involved in the minutia and the daily details of our personal lives, because even though he is God of the universe, little ol' we still (and especially) matter to *Him*.

So many of us feel insignificant, unworthy, and unappreciated or undervalued, and it's hard for them to believe God would even care. So many of us think no one cares, but God absolutely does. Why do we expect the gods we created to seemingly take care of and provide for us? We usually must buy them to use them to help us in the first place. Why do we love how they make us feel in those quick moments? Unfortunately, those moments disappear all too quickly. Then we must buy more, or use more, or have more of a substance that can maim or kill us. They can destroy our physical, mental, and emotional state and, even more so, distort our spirituality. In fact, these manmade idols are utterly worthless. Those of us who know the Heavenly Father and know Him well are not exempt from the stumbling blocks listed above. For most of us, idolatry can come in more subtle ways, such as "works" (that's a Christianese word for doing stuff to get noticed by God and man; how much you do or how much you give is contingent on how much you hope to be seen in the church). Hey, did everyone see that? I can write this because I personally know about this because I've done some of these very things myself.

For some, it is comparing yourself to others to the point of jealousy—that's just sad but oh so true, just sayin'. It's challenging, like, "Why can't I do that like brother or sister so-and-so?" instead of praying for our own anointing and not worrying about "a performance." You know, like bragging about how "I sang that song like no one else" instead of worshipping. Side note: Worship is not ever about a song you sing but the life you live glorifying the Heavenly Father. Having a relationship with God the Father, His Son, and the Holy Spirit is vital for a healthy spiritual and physical life. Being led by His voice is critical. Some of us have sought the accolades of men, and most of us do so without sincerely ever realizing it. Using His word, which is good, freeing, and full of direction and loving guidance, let's acknowledge that as the truth and our truth.

Now, back to my MINI. Here comes the best part! You no longer need the accolades of any man or woman; you never did. Once you realize this, you get to choose to change and realize no man ever needed to approve of you. All you'll ever need is the loving, approving acceptance of the one who created you, the One who doesn't want you to exist without Him. Why would you ever so desperately need anyone else for approval for anything? I am not saying for us not to listen to Mom and Dad, or our teachers and laws, rules, and regulations. We still must honor those who are in authority. We are and can be children of the One True God, Our Father. He is not a god we created, but He is the God who *created us*! Now choose for yourself either the temporary accolades of man or the eternal blessed approval of *God*. Choose wisely!

~MEDITATION MOMENTS ~

Little children, keep yourselves from idols.(1 John 5:21, ESV).

"You can safely assume that you've created God in your own image when it turns out that God hates all the same people you do." Anne Lamott.

"Everyone should be respected as an individual, but no one idolized." Albert Einstein

~PRAYER ~

Father God in heaven, thank You for showing me Your unconditional love. Thank You, that through You I can accept myself for who and how You've created me. I can now choose to be everything You've always wanted me to be. To be all that I can be without comparisons, jealousies, inadequacies, or inferiorities. Through You, I can be the wonderful creation You have made me to be. You've made me part of a loving and caring generation to show light and love without judgment. Thank You for enlightening me through Your amazing living *word*! In Jesus's name, *amen*.

~YOUR PRAYER OR THOUGHTS FOR TODAY ~

Mini Read 11

If I Lived in This World

My Personal Rant! If I lived in this World (here is what I would do) although I am "not of it"

For starters, if I lived in this world, I wouldn't go around speeding on the highways, byways, or freeways while giving some law-abiding citizen the evil eye or, worse, the middle finger. I've seen it done. I wouldn't talk about my neighbors behind their backs. If I lived in this world, I wouldn't allow the innocent to be taken advantage of, even if it meant I turned out not to be the most popular person because of my stand on what I know is right to do. If I lived in this world, I would go around doing kind things for complete and total strangers but also and especially for my very own family and friends; and yes, even those who would call themselves my enemies. If I lived in this world.

If I lived in this world, I would make sure I did my best at all times even and especially when I knew there was no one watching me, just because. If I lived in this world, I would go around doing not just random acts of kindness but acts of kindness and paying it forward. If I lived in this world, I would go around doing the right thing even if those around me would not. If I lived in this world, I would live a life full of love, kindness, patience, goodness, self–control, peace, joy, faithfulness, and gentleness. I would support my friends and family who were successfully doing things I could not do without being jealous of them. I would give them unconditional love and support! If I lived in this world.

If I lived in this world, I would try a little tenderness every day, and try to give to others what I would so desperately need and want for myself. If I lived in this world, I would give respect, honor, attentiveness, time, and love—mostly love. If I lived in this world, I would go around smiling just because I woke up that day. If I lived in this world, I would treat all of the inhabitants I came across—you know, other humans—with such care, as if someone greater than myself had placed each and every one of them there on purpose somehow. If I lived in this world, I would try to do unto others as I honestly would want them to do unto me! If I lived in this world, I would go around trying to make a difference for the good of those around me, just for the fun of it. If I lived in this world.

You know, if I lived in this world, I would look for beauty inside of every person I came across, regardless or race, creed, color, sex, or whatever. If I lived in this world, I would try to be as accepting of others as I would want them to be of me. I would do so even if we didn't see eye to eye on who our political choices were. If I lived in this world, I would do my best to walk in forgiveness, mercy, and grace, the way I would want it for myself. If I lived in this world, I would allow folks the freedom of not living from their past but prayerfully learning from it and moving on. If I lived in this world.

If I lived in this world, I think I would be one of those cheesy, corny, faith-filled, real-loving, follow-our-Holy-leader type of Christians. You know the ones who love like He did, and does, without judgment but with character and integrity. If I lived in this world, I would go around saying what He said and says, without beating folks down or over their heads but by building them up with those encouraging, beautiful written words! If I lived in this world, I would express His awesomeness and share the freedom and continued liberty only He offers. If I live in this world.

If I lived in this world—though clearly, I am not of it—I would do and try my best to introduce as many Pre-Cs that would hear me, one by one or by the hundreds, to the love and joy He can give no matter who, no matter what, no matter how old or young, no matter where they came from or have been, no matter what they may have done. If I lived in this world, I would introduce those folks to *Him*! That is, if I lived in this world!

~Meditation Moment~

And he said to him, "You shall love the Lord your God with all your heart and with all your soul and with all your mind. 38 This is the great and first commandment. 39 And a second is like it: You shall love your neighbor as yourself.(Matt. 22:37–39, ESV).

"Spread love everywhere you go. Let no one ever come to you without leaving happier." Mother Teresa

~Prayer for Today~

Heavenly Father, it is clear that we do live in this world, so I ask Papa God, how would You have me live my life for *You* today? Help me be an example to Pre-Cs! Help me to share without being mean, crude, or harsh—to share that everyone has the potential to be a true follower of Jesus Christ! Even in my mistakes, please allow me the opportunity to demonstrate what the word *Christian* means. Asking for and offering forgiveness for myself and extending that same thing to others who may have offended or hurt me. Bless me to be a true ambassador of heaven, as I live in this world.

Mini Read 11

~YOUR PRAYER OR THOUGHTS FOR TODAY~

Mini Read 12

The Freedom of Forgiveness
The Freedom of Forgiveness: I can't let it go!

(Inspired by one of my intergenerational and international BFFs, Lil J)

I am not sure what else needs to be said about forgiveness and the complete and total freedom that comes with it. Well, except this: Why is it so freaking hard to forgive in the first place? Right? After living through a horrible event or experience, after speaking with others, this is what I have heard and learned . . .

. . . *well,* I tell you what, sometimes I just don't feel like it, like the person that just did me wrong needs to know they were wrong and I am feeling justified in my anger and attitude toward them for the ill treatment. I get to make sure that you, the perpetrator, must now pay for the hurt that was inflicted upon me all of those years, months, days, weeks, and, yes, even hours ago; that thing hurt, and for some of us, myself included, it still does! My tears and frustration at the stupidity, the arrogance that they felt to deal that hurt to me is blinding my heart from recovery. I am overwhelmed with a feeling of internal combustion! It didn't even seem to matter to them; they didn't even seem to care. And for them, yes, they seemed to even enjoy the horrific pain and suffering they inflicted upon me. My heart hurts from this, you know! You, you, you *jerk* or *jerkette*, if the shoe fits! How could one human being inflict such suffering or pain on another? Would you want that done to you? Listen to me; I am asking you a question here. I can't seem to let it go!

And you know what else? They never once said, or probably will ever say, that "they are sorry." Oh, woe is me, woe is me indeed. I am just sick to my stomach over this whole thing; I just can't seem to let it go. And look at them over there living their lives to fullest, enjoying themselves, having fun. What the flip is this? And then look at me over here; I am still seething on the inside, making myself sick! I am filled with anger and rage over what was done to me, or over what was said. I am just *sick*! Some of us will actually get sick, allergies, skin conditions, constant migraines, arthritis, and intestinal issues, and even cancer. With that being said, read on, please; I implore you.

Someone once said to me—she is full of great wisdom, but at the time I felt like she had the gall to say this to me—"What if that person who caused you harm or pain never apologizes? You have to ask yourself one very important question." "Okay," I said, "I'll bite. What is the question?" She said, "Will you be all right?" I was like, "Lady are you frickin' crazy? Do you know what they did to me? It was awful, it was horrible, it wasn't right, it was for some of us inhuman, it wasn't fair!" Now fair is a whole other story, I found out later. She said, "No, I don't know what they did, and you are right in saying life isn't fair, but there is justice and injustices, and you get to choose! You get to choose how you will live the rest of your life." Just so y'all know, I really don't like the C word: *choose*. It feels like a four-letter word to me sometimes: choose, chose, choice—I hate that word in all its forms, seriously! . . . "You can forgive them she said, and commence your healing process, and began to come back into your own prominence, and prosperity, your own joy, living your life to the fullest extent possible. You can allow your heart to be healed and set free from the dark hold this un-forgiveness had and has on you and know it may be a process, maybe for a while daily, but a healthy one."

. . . Then it hit me like smacking into a brick wall on a bicycle like a cartoon character—forgiveness doesn't take the perpetrator off the hook; it releases me and you from the anger, the guilt, the shame, the frustration, the invisible personal prison that you or I may be living in. Completely devoid of living or life or joy and happiness, the ability to explore or be "me" or "you" freely! And then like the Grinch after almost destroying Whoville on Christmas morning, it gave me the ability to grow my heart three sizes in one day! I then realized that no matter what I did, this person just might go on living their life, completely and fully unaware, without any regrets, and my anger aimed at them would not stop them, their days and life would go on, and without a mere thought of me, but that by me forgiving them, I would release "me."

Well, maybe my heart didn't grow three sizes that day, but it sure felt like it; with this revelation, my heart did change, and so did my stinkin' thinkin'. Be careful when reading this, because we all probably have at least one of these circumstances in our lives to deal with. Here's what you want to be careful of, though—is that each one of us on some level could have been the perpetrator to someone else. Just sayin' forgiveness releases you into complete *freedom*! Oh happy day, happy day, you washed my tears away! So forgiveness is a great release for you the broken, the hurt, the living in pain; remember the person who hurt you is not off the hook unless they go to the Creator to seek His forgiveness for themselves, and then we get to give that one over to Him. *Freedom!*

~Meditation Moments~

Beloved, never avenge yourselves, but leave it to the wrath of God, for it is written,"Vengeance is mine, I will repay, says the Lord." (Rom. 12:19, ESV).

"Forgiveness is just another name for freedom." Byron Katie

~Prayer for Today~

Heavenly Father, thank You for this day, and thank You that Your forgiveness is free for the asking, literally. Your word says that if we confess with our mouths, You are quick and just to forgive us our sins—our missing it, not getting it right, missing the mark, so to speak. I ask You now for forgiveness. Your word tells us it is a command to forgive, so I choose to do just that! Bless me now to forgive those who I believe and know have wronged me. Bless me to release them into your more-than-capable and loving hands not to destroy them but to allow them this very same blessed freedom you have now given to me! Bless your holy and magnificent name in Jesus's name. Amen!

~YOUR PRAYER OR THOUGHTS FOR TODAY~

Mini Read 13

The Weirdest Lonely I Have Ever Known
(Inspired by my dad passing away)

Death has a strange way of causing us to take a long look at life sometimes. To reflect and remember days long since gone. At least death has for me. You see my dad had passed away a few days before I wrote this. And I had a mixed bag of emotions going through my mind and my body. My spirit man was at peace; that's how it is when you have a deep, meaningful relationship with the Creator, God! I was all but unsettled in my heart over the loss of my dad.

You see, my siblings and I did not always have our dad in our lives growing up. I know—same old story for so very many of us, right? Except I am happy to say most of us are no long bitter or angry or disrespectful of who he was to us. You know what, I'll just speak for myself going forward. My interactions with my dad were not always the best, nor the worst, nor was he the best or worst dad ever. He was not abusive, but because he was not there for protection, there was abuse, at least for me.

You see, in his youth when we were still just younglings, my dad was very selfish and self-absorbed. His drugs, fancy cars, and pretty women were what he was after—at least that's what I remember. My mom was one beautiful and gorgeous lady, so I don't get that!

My dad was encouraged by his mom, my grandmother, to forsake his family and just come home to her, and she would take care of him. What the hell was that? Hey, y'all, don't worry—the word *hell* is in the Bible. Back to my story, do you know that woman didn't even acknowledge us after that? Relevant side note here: I live by the good book, which I was taught to live by and believe, but I was also taught not to be so heavenly minded that I became no earthly good. Be kind, thoughtful, respectful, and always loving. Man, if we just walked in the kind of love the Creator desires, all would be well. Anywho, back to my regularly scheduled MINI/story.

There were times, because of his absence, we only hand bologna sandwiches, with sugar water instead of a ten-cent pack of red Kool-Aid. There were times my mom worked three or four different jobs, and me being the oldest, I was a latchkey kid before the term was ever made known or became a thing. I could go on and on about all the things we missed out on because of my dad's absence, but that's not where this is going.

My brothers and sister and I grew up rich in ways that money could not ever provide. We have full and colorful memories of times gone by when family and a simple Sunday evening meal meant everything. We grew up understanding it was cool to hang out with your mom, brothers, sisters, cousins— well, you get the point. We told elaborate stories by using our imagination, vision, and insights. We sang silly songs together while going to visit our cousins in the next town over in our

"Flintstone mobile" (for some of you younger folks, Google it!). Sometimes we slept on the floor in the only room that had the only square floor fan, or box fan for some of y'all, in it to keep us all cool at night. We learned how to handle our differences with dignity and honor, and we learned character. We learned that money doesn't make you rich, but true and precious love does.

I guess where I am going with this is, I feel sorry for my dad, because it was he who missed out on all of that. You see, although our lives were a struggle as times, we powered through and blamed no one for our situation or circumstance in life. The same life back then that was difficult and sometimes harsh is the same life I wouldn't trade for all the gold in China, or wherever all the gold is these days. My dad missed out on the family life we got to share with our mama—that woman, woo, but then that's another story. Ooooh-weee, my mom—I'm laughing out loud to myself right now and almost rolling on the floor. Let me just say, my mom was no joke; sometimes I just called her Miss Rose. Maybe I'll tell you all about her sometime, 'cause you didn't mess with Miss Rose, y'all. "squirrel moment"!!!

Well, my dad did show up some thirty-odd years later in our lives. My brother found him, but he showed up on my doorstep. He was an old man by then, and I did not recognize him when I went to the airport to pick him up. Life had not been so kind to him I could see. He was humbled by time, by people who had not treated him well, by life itself. Life had been brutal to him in so many ways. I tell you, as angry as I had been with him down through the years, when I saw him standing there, afraid to even approach me, my heart, oh my heart couldn't just be angry anymore. And all the forgiveness I didn't know I had within me came flooding out of me. All the bitterness began to melt away and just slide off like greased slime on the back of a wet duck!

I walked over to him and reached for him, and my dad fell over in my arms and cried like a baby, and so did I. I immediately introduced him to my children, and gingerly we began a new chapter in our lives that forever changed us all.

Let's fast-forward to the present. We just laid him in the ground just yesterday at the time of me writing this part of the story. And do you know what I found in Dad's funeral service? Grace, mercy, forgiveness, redemption. Who would have thought that a man who lived such a wild and crazy life could find such a thing, but he did; he found redemption through the blood of our Savior! He found his peace, his hope, and he had faith in God! It was the blood that saved the beast, Jesus's blood. Now I know a lot of years of forgiveness, healing, kindness, and patience are omitted from this story. But I will tell you this: It was God, and His glorious Son, who did it, and allowed us all to participate in this time of redemption. It is the same blood that reached out and down through the years to and for us all. Now I am not writing to offend any of the nonbelievers who read this. I am not going to try and bully anyone into believing in God. Besides, I have found that when we live our lives as we are called to, truth defends and defines itself. Besides, folks don't want to know how much you know until they know how much you care! But I will not be ashamed of the Gospel that has saved me and saved my dad! The true and real-life experiences I have lived are sometimes spectacular, to say the least. I would love to share one or two with y'all in the days to come.

Let me share this: I found a peace I had never known and would not have if I had not gone at least to honor the man God choose to be my earthly father. I tell you, the way he lived the last years of his life is enough to make one cry tears of joy. I have a peace and love for my earthly dad, and my Heavenly Father, I would not have been able to comprehend, or to share in. I finally understand that one parable in the Bible where the boss gives the same wage to the ones who worked from morning until the end of the workday in the fields as he did to those precious souls who only worked that last hour. My dad's life, and how he lived those end days, was a gift to all who got to know him. He was honored by the military as if he were a five-star general, and by the few who attended as if he were a saint, a son of God, a quiet general for the kingdom of heaven, because that is who he was and now is.

No longer do I feel sad or sorry for my dad! Nor am I angry, bitter, or full of regret. I am proud and honored God chose that man to be my dad; he was and is a gift to me and my siblings. Thank You, God, for showing the redemptive love of the Lamb through the life of my earthly father. It is You who gives peace and allows us all to know how much You love us. As my brother told me before he took me to the airport, one of the last things our dad said, with tears streaming down his face, was, "I know that God loves me." I am a child of God.

Me too, Daddy, me too! I still feel lonely, and it's still weird, but now I get it. The weirdest lonely one can feel is missing someone who never leaves your heart and who's waiting on the beautiful other side of this life.

Dedicated to the memory of my loving, imperfect dad!

~Meditation Moments~

For my thoughts are not your thoughts, neither are your ways my ways, declares the Lord. (Isa. 55:8, ESV).

Your way, O God is holy. What God is great like our God? (Ps. 77:13, ESV).

"The successful man will profit from his mistakes and try again in a different way." Dale Carnegie

Prayer for today:

Heavenly Father, sometimes Your plans for us just don't make sense to our finite minds; they are beyond our earthly comprehension. I thank You for Your loving hand in my life, even when I would not have chosen the path You did for my life. I am stronger, smarter, and hopefully getting continuously wiser because of it. Thank You for giving my dad the opportunity and choice to seek You out for himself as his own Lord and Savior. Thank You for receiving him. Thank You, God, for being God in our lives. It is a gift and an honor to be Your child. Giving You all the praise, honor, and glory in Jesus's name! Amen.

~YOUR PRAYER OR THOUGHTS FOR TODAY~

Mini Read 14

I Almost Didn't Finish
Feeling All the Feels I Felt! (includes "Super Minis")
Why Not Just Quit?

Feeling the Ish of It All

Let me tell you something: I don't know of anyone who hasn't gone through "ish" in their lives. I think sometimes USNs, well, we can become complacent and do not want to deal with the reality and accept the fact that we get hit and hurt just like "everyone else." What I mean by that is those who appear to be outside of the promises of God are a covenant for the learned ones. Sometimes we USNs get a little haughty and place ourselves above the "rest"! Y'all know what I mean? I also think those outside of those promises, whether by ignorance or those who choose not to believe, sometimes think that USNs don't have to deal with some of the same crappy things that "they" do (or at least so I've been told by some). Hey now, Christ followers get sick and have financial issues and hardships; have bad days on the road, at work, at home; lose family and friends; our children get sick or hurt. We have issues in our marriages, and sadly sometimes even get divorced. We have "ish" too. So stop thinkin' that stupid crap!

I am so flippin' tired of folks thinking that being a follower of Christ, another term for Christian, by the way, is about being perfect or perfection. Well, it isn't; it's messy sometimes. It's seemingly illogical; it feels upside down and inside out—just crazy! Being a follower is a lot of times going against everything that the world seems to deem as normal. You give money to get money. Actually that isn't quite correct; it should go more like "You got blessed so you get to give." Taught by my current pastor, I can vibe with that; you forgive to be free of being wronged, you get to love your neighbor and accept them despite their being different. You exchange faith for fear in your fellow man, meaning mankind, not excluding anyone here. You place others above and before yourself, and unconditional love of all others is absolutely *key*! Being a follower of the One who is "the Way" is not for the faint of heart! It's hard a lot of times. You have to be able to take a punch or two. When people say Christianity or being a follower of Christ is the easy way out of life, that it's a crutch, I can personally tell you that's a bunch of bull doo-doo! I know then they don't comprehend the "narrow path" that means taking the high road and doing it with Jesus by all way for all of you who didn't know. All that being said, I have found that eventually it's worth the work and the effort. Because when you are going through some nasty doo-doo, dung, poo-poo, ish, you are probably like me—you want out in week three of a five-week process (and by the way, no one ever lets you in on how long the process is or could be; you just have to trust in the One, meaning have faith), because it may feel like a hellacious mess! One may or may not see at the time that you will come through it all right as long as you keep your focus on the One who never loses a fight (a battle for the religious), but I am sharing with you it is really the truth (insert smiley face here).

Feels Like This, Y'all

This part is extremely personal to me. Sometimes even as a Christian you do not come out unscathed, and neither did I on this one, y'all. Sometimes and a lot of times there will be battle scars. But rarely does one die from a scar alone! I tell you this from experience. Ooowee child, that being said, God help me! I wanted to scream, and I am sure I did through these last few months or so! They were so hard and challenging. It would seem the closer I got to finishing this assignment, the more challenging and difficult my life became. Hey now, can I get a what-what! You'll see what I mean as you read on—and please do read on! You see, it's what we choose to do with our circumstances; it is our faith and belief in our good, good God, because in almost every instance, it is our faith and belief that the enemy is actually challenging! But I am here to tell you that our God will always come through for us. So far, for me and my household, God always has come through. Mind you, not like I planned and/or dreamt. Let's call it what it really is, y'all—I "fantasized" about how my situation might ought to go, and God goes, "Nope, that's not it, my love." Sometimes I do believe God thinks He's in charge, and I should just follow Him and His plan . . . might be easier, that's for sure!

Feeling Angry

Those of us who think we know the word of God, the Bible, should remember this:

We do not fight against flesh and blood; you know real live living people; they are not our true enemies. However, these same people are choosing to follow a negative unction, whether it is by listening to the dark side of humanity, very similar to the dark side of the force. like *Star Wars*, or they have allowed their minds and hearts to be emotionally and/or spiritually altered, once again in a negative way. So although it may seem and feel like it sometimes, because you want to slap them like they are real enemies. Because they might be all up in our faces, talking smack, being incredibly mean, difficult, and harsh. Some are just wicked and downright evil, cruel, and hard to live with or be around. They may even hate you! Personally, I find it hard to comprehend that one human being could show such awful actions toward another. But still, I want to remind you, we wrestle with an unseen force of evil, always trying to stop us, slow us down, make us quit, force us to throw in the towel, force us to become complacent, just giving you and I the opportunity to become apathetic, make it seem like it's our own idea to quit! Giving us crap when what we could sincerely use and need is a break! And that break does not seem to ever come! If you don't know, the enemy is morbidly relentless! He doesn't care that you're tired, doesn't care about your tears, and will enjoy hitting you while you're down, and bring his gang to keep the beating going while you are facedown in the dirt! Ever feel like that? It is like a demonic gang beating.

Feeling the Fight!

Know and understand this: On a cosmic level, the Enemy is looking to destroy God's people, and I tell you this much I have learned. We, being USNs, may not think too much of ourselves, or we may not see our own "true" potential of who we really are in Christ! But hear me: somehow the glimpse that the Enemy got of the amazing plans the One, our good *God* has for us—to prosper us; bless us; give us victory in every circumstance and situation; and allow us to bless others along the paths of our lives—well, that was enough for the Enemy to try to take us all out using whatever he could find to confound us, distract us, keep us unfocused, get us to feel sorry for ourselves. Because things haven't turned out the way we thought. Fight back; fight back with God's good word! Learn it, study it, listen to it, get it down for yourself! Live it! You heard me—just do it! It works!

Humph, I say tell that old devil, "I'm not listening to you or your gnarly, nasty lies, you frickin' poo-head. You go to hell, you creep!" What I am about to say may sound counterproductive here, but pray. Pray for your adversary/your enemies—yes, sincerely pray for them. Also, the other key—and this one pissed me off for realz—"Forgive them!" When I got that little whisper in my head from God, I almost said, "Get thee behind me Satan!" That's Christianese for "You've got to be kidding me, man!" What the fruitbat!

You know what else I have found? The folks the enemy chooses to use—well, it's just not quite right. That poo-head can sometimes work through those closest to you, those who you have let in and who have gotten close to your heart. A best friend, spouse, coworker, boss, and, yes, occasionally a stranger. But I guess the poo-head devil isn't ever going to play fair. Why would he be kind and start now, and use someone who is sincerely an enemy you could and would recognize right away? You know like in the movies, where they wear all black and have horns on their heads. Well, for me I think that person the enemy used was wearing all black, and I know for sure I saw horns sticking out of the sides of their ... naw, naw that's just me being a little bit petty, I guess, and trying to be funny and add some humor to a really bad situation, huh. I'm probably the only one laughing here, I'm sure. My husband says I have bad timing with where to put my jokes, so even now it's probably bad timing. Hey, guys, I'm human too!

Side Feels

Let me share with you all what had happened since my original completion date was blown. I have been sick and had a diagnosis that was for me devasting! I mean, really, why now? The poo-head devil is like, "Why not now?" But my good, good Heavenly Father has already stated, "Don't even worry about it, girl! Don't even! It is not a concern for you! Hey, lady, try exercise, eat right, get yourself some good sleep. The way has already been made for you. Trust in the Lord!"

Those Marriage Feels, Though

Then let's not even talk about the attack on my marriage and relationship with my boo! I am being transparent here, folks—with his permission, of course. Just know the enemy is no joke! He will hit you below the belt in every way possible. Fight back with the good word of God! I cannot stress this enough! His Love, and be sure to know it is unconditional *love*, is the answer. Well, my boo and I finally hit an all-time low that stung us both in the face! And quickly, with the guidance and help of Godly counseling, we came running back to our God. Not that we ever really left; we just got sidetrack for a bit. We allowed family members to meddle in our very personal business. They spoke lies and deceit and denied it! But when you have a member of your close family determined to be a degenerate in your home, you almost don't stand a chance. It kept going for a couple of years but came to a head during the time I was getting close to completing this very project.

But God! Holy Hallelujah came through when one of us said, "We have got to stop this if we want to stay married and have a healthy relationship!" Thank the One above for my husband, because at the time, I was overwhelmed and was like, "I'm done, damn it!" Just done with it all. No, y'all, it wasn't me who was willing to fight for us anymore. You see, this is my second go-round in marriage, and I was getting tired fast and had seen all this bull doo-doo crap, or just plain BS, before and I was over it and done. But my husband wasn't about to let it be like that. I am so grateful, because I was basing our relationship on what I had experienced before rather than what "the good word" said! God used a spiritual defibrillator to jolt us back into reality. Once my husband got me to refocus and calm down, I was able to see our relationship for the blessing and gift it was always intended to be. Because our marriage is not just about us alone! Nobody's marriage is; nobody's marriage is ever only about two people, but in those moments, it had to be in order to heal.

Basically, we then got the godly guidance we needed to save our marriage, and our relationship! It's okay to get help, y'all! It is okay that you may be in over your head and realize it, and to look for wise people who are grounded in "the good word." Who understand the stresses and marital challenges that come to some. Or that you may need help in other areas of your life, just make sure these are folks who will give sound Godly guidance and advice. That's what me and my boo did! This is why we are still standing today! A beautiful shout-out to our incredible counselors! You two folks rock! Seriously, by the blessings and grace of God, we are still standing together, strong with God at the center of all we are and do! You go, God!

Messing with Family Feels—Our Children

Then on top of that, once I decided to return and go ahead and complete this first major project, one of my children got sick! She had a stroke, and that almost took me out for sure. She was in her early thirties at that time, so what the heck. I was devastated in every way! As a parent, you just can't make sense of your beautiful gifts from "Heaven" Himself hurting, down, and out. I mean, when you understand that every life given is an eternal gift from the One! I felt helpless; I felt numb on the inside and outside of my body. I couldn't think that awful day. My poor child was lying in a hospital bed, unable to speak or be coherent enough to speak my name! She couldn't even remember her own. But let me share with you the miraculous love and power of that day, if you will. She had just started a new job, and her new boss had said, "Don't worry about coffee for tomorrow. I will be getting coffee and breakfast for everyone." Awesome boss, right? Still, she found herself at the coffee shop. Somehow, she left her phone and her watch at home in her bed, probably because she had already started to feel wonky and weird. But she got to the coffee shop, which was just five to ten minutes from the hospital, and she didn't need to go to the coffee shop in the first place, remember. As she got to the counter, she started losing the ability to speak, she became lightheaded, and she fainted; she hit the floor, I was told. Thankfully she was in a coffee shop where EMTs, nurses, and doctors frequent.

They immediately took action and started working with her and getting an ambulance to get her to the hospital right up the hill from where they were. Apparently, they were able to get her there in record time. Once there, the nurse said it took about two hours before my daughter could state, "Call my mom," and became coherent enough to give them the correct phone number. They called and left a voice mail on my phone because I was at work. Now, generally I don't bother to listen to voice mails for quite a while when I am at work, and if I don't recognize the number, for sure, but this time I had that special tingling, for lack of a better term—a "spider sense" that told me to take a moment to listen. When I did, I was like, "Oh my God, *no!*" I called and confirmed the information the nurse left and was at the hospital in about fifteen minutes. Honestly, that is not humanly possible, but I did it, and I got no tickets. There was almost no traffic, but I am still unaware of just how I did that. But I tell you this a "follower of Christ" But God, won't he do it" won't he do it. Once I got there, I can't tell you the personal agony and pain I felt seeing my child lying there helpless and scared. As she came to, looked up, and saw me, the only thing she could say, with tears flowing down her cheeks and fear in her eyes, was, "Mom, my words; I can't find my words." It took all that I had as a mother and as a Christian—as a human being—not to lose it right there in front of her, but somehow, I held it together and told her everything was going to be all right.

Feeling the Presence in Hard Times

I could say yes to that, because I was already praying before I walked in the room. As a "follower of Christ," you learn early on when you pray according to His "good word," it is already answered, and to trust and believe in that. One more thing about that day: Before anyone else arrived to see her, I got to a place I could not think anymore. I cried out in my mind, but once in her room, I just froze. Anyway, I began to sing, in sounds and utterances. For those of you who know what I mean: "singing in the spirit." I thought I was just singing over my child. But the nurses on duty said whatever I was singing, there came a hush in the emergency room, everything stopped, and everyone who could hear listened, and there was a peacefulness for a few minutes. People were calmed by the sound of my voice, and although I sang not one recognizable word, my daughter said she heard and understood all the words I sang. I share this with you, the reader, because God can use us in wonderful and mysterious ways. Even when we are unaware and just doing what we know to do, being humbled by life; and in this case, I was crying out to the One whom I love and who loves me and mine for help in the only way I knew how in that moment. He used my cry, my song, my voice to bring a peace to a whole emergency room, if only for a few minutes, and assurance to my child, because I believe she heard God's blessings and promises that she was going to be all right!

Well, even though she had a stroke, within twenty-four hours she was released; to this day, her neurologists cannot explain the miraculous full and complete recovery she made. One neurologist got down on her knees and looked in my daughter's face, analyzing every detail, and said, "How are you talking to me?" "How are you eating, chewing and swallowing, and how are you even laughing, because her brother got jokes, so soon after this event?" They had to release her, because they could find no reason to keep her in the hospital any longer. That is what is known to many as a bona fide miracle. Now, she is still under medical care, and being medically supervised closely by a great team of doctors and nurses. But she is now living her life to the fullest degree of her God-given ability. Oh, how grateful I am, but I tell you, I almost quit, because when the enemy comes after your children, there is a helplessness one can feel that can take you out. I tell you, I almost quit this whole thing, and just when I thought I could do this again and pull myself together. Well, please read on. The ish really hit the fan.

This Doesn't Feel So good

Then you guys, through all of this, I had a family member personally verbally attack me again and again, continuously, relentlessly, without mercy, without remorse! Just mean and vengeful. I felt like they wanted to see me destroyed and see me taken out. They used their own personal anger, hurts, and fears to insert themselves into places of my life they had no damn business! I felt like their foot was on my neck and I couldn't breathe, I couldn't move; I felt helpless! Remember I said earlier we don't fight against real, live, living people but against wicked, sick, evil entities? Well, although this statement is true per the written word of *God*, also keep this in mind: some of these folks open themselves up to being used by the enemy, the devil. How, you might ask? Well, by never letting go of their own past hurts and fears; never letting go of their own pain, their own anger; holding on to their disappointments; by being angry with God and never allowing forgiveness to take hold in their hearts! I've seen it in my life and in the lives of others. I have even seen it when an event doesn't go our way at times. We blame anyone else or any other thing rather than realizing we may have made some busted-up and bad choices or life is just sometimes like that. You do everything you know to do, and still nothing goes your way. Hey, everyone, always remember, though, through it all God is still on His throne. Meaning He has got this and God has got you Boo! In many cases, however, so many people choose to blame the One when it was, in fact, a person who chose to hurt them. That mean ol' buttmunch of a human being chose to cause you harm or do you wrong. You see, guys, there are those who are not going to like you even if you have done nothing at all to them.

Not Even Your Own Feels, They Just Don't Like You Feels . . . Sadness

Then someone went out of their way to ensure they didn't like me because I was different than they were. You see, maybe you were born a person of color or maybe you were not; maybe you were born male or female. Maybe to them it's just the fact that you were born at all. Unfortunately, those types of folks exist, and sadly—oh, so very sadly—sometimes we ourselves are acting like or being those folks. It's a scary thing, isn't it, when we also need to look in the mirror? Personally, I loathe that part of myself—discovery! However, please keep this in mind: you can make a different choice. Know why? You can choose! Sometimes that just pisses me off! Sometimes I get mad at God for that! I just want God to hit the "do as I say" button and not give me the ability to ruin not just my life but, terrifyingly, maybe someone else's. Still, "Our Beautiful Creator" will not ever override someone's free will, meaning the gift to decide for themselves. But if we ask for His help, He is faithful, trustworthy, and tried and true to come through. We can never ask for the One to make someone to stop hurting us or to "make" them do what we think said person should do. He cannot even make us choose Him, even unto eternal death.

Feeling Your Right to Choose

You see, God will give you the honor of not choosing Him all the way to hell. The honor of choice is always yours. That's why it is not our place to force our thoughts, our desires, or our will on anyone else, either. If God does not or will not force anyone to choose Him, again, neither should we force or manipulate anyone into choosing God; only kindly show them the path to God! But when we do ask Him to help us, when we ask Him, well, that empowers Him to do just that. Listen, even if you are ignorant to this fact of choice, it still will not negate his written word, God will not override anyone's freedom of choice. God is not a bully! I tell you, sometimes for the sake of relationships, for peace, for life, you have to choose to give up your right to be right! Ask anyone who has ever been in a marriage! They will tell you this is truth. Still, God will allow you to make your own choice to choose to do what is right or wrong, to choose Him or not, all the way to your choosing hell over heaven! God does not want robots or Stepford wives.

So when those angry, bitter folks are doing what they do, know it is their choice to do so! That's some heavy "ish," y'all. Sounds like someone you may know. Does any of this sound like you? Guys, let that disgusting, infested buttmunch go! Forgive those people who have seriously done you wrong! I know—you've got to be kidding me, right? But I'm not! Remember forgiveness doesn't say what they did was all right, but it states they no longer have power over you or life. Seek out the One and allow him to walk you through it. I personally can say I have had to walk and live this one out a few times. It may take a daily walk of saying "I forgive you for what you did to me!" It ain't easy, but it does feel like, and is, an incredible form of freedom! It is the ultimate freedom! This feeling almost tripped me up and caused me to throw in the towel and just quit!

Feeling Unworthy

One thing I have found out since I have had the honor of living this life so far: no matter what, it is not about how awesome you are, how much you've got, or all that you have accomplished. If you don't treat others with love, respect, and honor, you are simply a hollow, empty trash bin. Because basically it is about your relationships—your relationships with God, family, and friends. How have you handled, and how do you handle, those relationships? Wait, do you have any relationships? How do you handle the "ish" and all that goes with it. Because honestly, right now, I am having an internal fight within myself. There are those in my life right now I just can't stand. I am doing my best to walk with God daily, because like the Hulk, I feel I am almost always angry. I hate this feeling. It can't be good; it's not what God wants for me, or for any of us. But sometimes we USNs need to be honest and share that sometimes we feel foul inside and we need His good word to walk us through. I admit that I need that right now in this moment, because I want to be better than this. I know one day soon, with the help of our good God and my good friends, this too shall pass. At least I'm working on it.

But honestly, I have felt unworthy to write lately. I have been ashamed of my anger and negativity. God, how can a Christian walk around like this? You see, our Heavenly Father asks you to take a look within and at yourself, to check your own heart. Check your own attitude. Who have you inadvertently judged or insulted, verbally bashed? For me, it was when I saw what I had done, what I had said, and those I had hurt, I fell to my knees in personal anguish and pain. I was appalled; I hated seeing that in myself. Just because I got hurt first. I asked God, "How could You use me?" And I believe He said to me, It's because you are willing to allow me in; you are a little bit broken right now." You see, I believe God uses the broken, because now that you understand what it's like to be butt-hurt to the core of your very being, you are more capable of helping someone else. I believe that when any USNs think we are all right, that we've got this, or we have a "nothing wrong with me" attitude, that is when you're probably not all right.

Only the Creator's love gives me what I need to complete each day. I almost didn't finish is an understatement. As a matter of fact, I am still walking this whole thing out as I am writing this. Sometimes there are no options to turn back; you are driving up the side of a cliff, and the mountain is to your left, even though there are guardrails to your right, you must focus on just moving forward, because there are no places to turn around. My only option, in my opinion, is to keep moving forward, or I could hold up traffic, because whether I realize it or not, somebody is following only God knows why, but I can't hold them up because of own personal insecurities and pain. I know with God all things are possible, so I move on in and through Him by faith. Because in every situation in my whole entire life, He has never once failed me. Nothing like I thought, or I dreamed it could or would be, or fantasized about, oh my goodness, y'all "but God"! So good; so, so very good. So I tell you now, trusting in our Beautiful Savior and wonderful Creator is the only way to finish this endeavor or anything else the Creator gives me. I still ask, "Can I finish this?"

God Feels Are Best!

I found out that not only does love cover a whole bunch of wrong stuff, like forgiveness and anger, it releases you from the agony of the pain of a past you can never change, you can never redo, not even one moment, and yet you may be still holding on to it. Let it go; leave it where it is! Let those folks go who hurt you; let go and let God do His thing. Let go of your boo-boos and mistakes; "drop it like it's a hot potato." You won't have to lift a finger—no, not one. You won't have to defend or vindicate yourself or speak up to redeem your innocence; I promise you God and time are on your side. Let love by your answer. Let all of that stupid junk go! Leave it, right now, again drop it, I'm telling you right now. Stop arguing with yourself, because Baby, I can't tell you the freedom and gift of peace that belongs to you, when you do this thing called forgiveness. Well, it is immeasurable. So, just drop that terrible awful stuff right now, once and for all! God's feels are wonderful!

Hey, guys, I almost didn't finish this, my first major assignment, because I had all these things and more coming against me. But here I am, and here you are reading this, my last story, for this, my first book. I chose to fight all that came against me and my family and friends. The desire I felt God placed in my heart was so overwhelming I couldn't not choose but to finish it! I hope and pray that if you have something you feel you're supposed to be doing, that if you have a dream that is big in your heart, I am here to tell you, don't allow anything or anyone to get you off track, certainly not the poo-head devil! Because my God—hopefully your God too, by now—is for you; you got this in Him! Now, just go get 'er done! I did, and I am no more special than you, the reader, reading this! Whooooohoooo!

Feeling Delayed, or Is It God's Timing?

My detours and delays were not to stop me in the way I thought those things and people were; now I understand that God wanted me to see it is in Him, who gives the dreams, who sustains them. It doesn't matter who or what circumstance may come, because as all of us USNs know, with God all things are possible, and also, He is so, so good to complete His good, magnificent work in me and my life, and yours too! So to with each of you, especially if you also choose Him. I tell you too, don't focus on what didn't happen but look to the future that our Heavenly Father, our Papa God, has for you! Because what may have seemed like an unfortunate delay or detour may have been our Heavenly Papa maneuvering you, not manipulating like humans do, but again I say maneuvering you into position for your gain and for His glory, in a future yet unseen and unexperienced. Because that is what life is all about! And boy do I have a story to share with all y'all, but that one has yet to be written!

~Meditation Moments~

Blesed be the God and the Father of our Lord Jesus Christ, the Father of mercies and God of all comfort,4 who comforts us in all our affliction, so that we may be able to comfort those who are in any affliction, with the comfort with which we ourselves are comforted by God. (2 Cor. 1:3-4, ESV)

"If you're going through hell, keep going." Winston Churchill

~Prayer~

Heavenly Papa, bless me to not ever look to myself for the strength that I can only find in You. Bless me to be a follower of Your word and to trust in it and to trust it, whether I understand it all or not. Papa God, continue to work in me the dreams and visions and assignments You have placed in my heart. Bless me to choose to forgive those who have discouraged me professionally, personally, and otherwise. Bless me to remember forgiveness does not take the person who hurt me off the hook for what they did, but it releases me from my past and propels me into the big and bright future You have for me. Papa God, thank You for being the truest form of *love* and allowing me to be an extension of that *love*! Thank You, Papa God, for seeing me as a complete and finished creation, being wonderfully and fearfully made in, by, and through You, in Jesus's name. Amen!

~WHAT IS YOUR PRAYER OR THOUGHTS FOR TODAY~